5.95

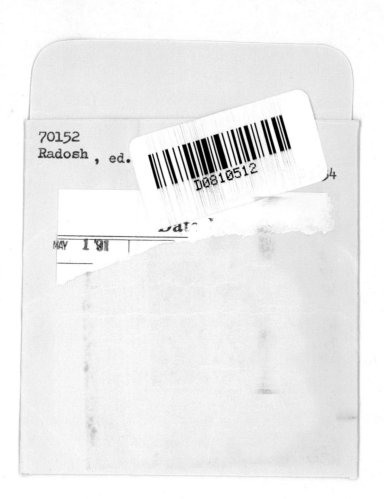

70152
Radosh , ed.

D0810512

MAY 1 '91

GREAT LIVES OBSERVED

Gerald Emanuel Stearn, *General Editor*

EACH VOLUME IN THE SERIES VIEWS THE CHARACTER AND
ACHIEVEMENT OF A GREAT WORLD FIGURE IN THREE PER-
SPECTIVES—THROUGH HIS OWN WORDS, THROUGH THE OPIN-
IONS OF HIS CONTEMPORARIES, AND THROUGH RETROSPECTIVE
JUDGMENTS—THUS COMBINING THE INTIMACY OF AUTOBI-
OGRAPHY, THE IMMEDIACY OF EYEWITNESS OBSERVATION,
AND THE OBJECTIVITY OF MODERN SCHOLARSHIP.

RONALD RADOSH *is Assistant Professor of History at Queens-
borough Community College, City University of New York.*

GREAT LIVES OBSERVED

Debs

Edited by **RONALD RADOSH**

The trouble with Debs is that he puts
the happiness of the race above everything else;
business, prosperity, property.

—LINCOLN STEFFENS

Debs knew of only one holy and,
from the standpoint of the proletariat, legal war,
namely: the war against the capitalists,
the war for the liberation of mankind from wage slavery.
I am not surprised that this fearless man
was thrown in prison by the American bourgeoisie.

—V. I LENIN

A SPECTRUM BOOK

PRENTICE-HALL, INC., ENGLEWOOD CLIFFS, N. J.

Current printing (last number): 10 9 8 7 6 5 4 3 2 1

C–13-197681-8

P–13-197673-7

Library of Congress Catalog Card Number: 75-140272

Printed in the United States of America

PRENTICE-HALL INTERNATIONAL, INC. (*London*)
PRENTICE-HALL OF AUSTRALIA, PTY. LTD. (*Sydney*)
PRENTICE-HALL OF CANADA, LTD. (*Toronto*)
PRENTICE-HALL OF INDIA PRIVATE LIMITED (*New Delhi*)
PRENTICE-HALL OF JAPAN, INC. (*Tokyo*)

Contents

v

PART THREE
DEBS IN HISTORY

GREAT LIVES OBSERVED

DEBS

Introduction

Eugene V. Debs was the most well known and highly regarded leader of the American Socialist party. A native midwesterner, Debs grew to adulthood as American capitalism was leaving laissez faire behind and developing into a mature corporate order. Debs was born in 1855, and when he was ready to find work, labor was scarce and jobs were plentiful. Railroad tracks were being laid throughout the nation, and like many other young men, Debs was able to find a job in this promising area. In his own home town of Terre Haute, Indiana, Debs gained his first experience with the workaday world as a railroad engine-house laborer.

Two years after he took his first job, Debs was promoted to locomotive fireman. He soon became a leader of the Brotherhood of Locomotive Firemen, the craft union representing his skill. But years of union effort brought little success. Railroad workers were divided along numerous craft lines and the corporations continued to grow at the laborer's expense. Debs's experience moved him to support the creation of an industrial union for all railroad labor, an organization that would "unify railroad employees" and "eliminate the aristocracy of labor."

The result was the birth in 1893 of the American Railway Union, a militant body that was to have early success by winning a massive strike against James J. Hill's Great Northern Railroad. But the strike waged against the Pullman Car Company was to have the greatest impact on Deb's future life.

George Pullman was widely known as a notorious opponent of organized labor. When hard times occur, Pullman once said, labor should suffer, since the worker contributes nothing to the success of a business enterprise. Operating according to this philosophy, Pullman between 1893 and May 1894 instituted harsh wage cuts on his line. But the workers who lived in his company town did not receive a corresponding decrease in their rent or food bills. When the ARU voted to strike, they were met with a Federal court injunction charging the union leaders with violation of the Sherman Anti-Trust Act of 1890, since a strike was held to be a conspiracy in restraint of trade. Federal troops were sent to Illinois to break the strike and Debs was arrested for violation of the injunction.

His six months in prison, at McHenry County Jail in Woodstock, Illinois, became a period of intense study and reflection for Debs. He

1

began to believe that his personal experience bore out the teachings of Karl Marx, that there was a class struggle going on in the capitalist United States. In prison Debs was often visited by Victor Berger, the eminent Marxist leader from Milwaukee, Wisconsin. He also read such Utopian works as Lawrence Gronlund's *The Co-Operative Commonwealth* and Edward Bellamy's *Looking Backward.* One of the earliest influences on Deb's thinking was a book he had read as a child, Victor Hugo's *Les Miserables.* In the novel, young Jean Valjean is forced to steal bread to feed his family. Debs began to realize that life was similar in his own country. Travels with railroad workers had taught him that injustice and poverty was rampant, and Hugo's descriptions of France became for Debs a mirror of the American reality. Dedicating himself to changing that reality, Debs became an exponent of a socialist commonwealth. The writings of the European Marxist Karl Kautsky, however, made the strongest impression on the young labor leader. Debs found Kautsky particularly "clear and conclusive," and his works enabled Debs to move "out of darkness into light."

From his emergence from Woodstock jail until his death in 1926, Eugene V. Debs was titular head of the American socialist movement, although by choice he stayed aloof from party politics and held no executive positions. As the best-known American socialist, Debs led the challenge that domestic radicals presented to the leaders of the new corporate capitalism. The corporate order, the socialists argued, had perhaps industrialized America and enriched a few. But it had failed to produce a community among the populace of America. A commonwealth at home could not be attained, they argued, on the foundation of a system based on private ownership of the means of production.

To create a new order, Debs argued that private property had to be abolished. Private property encouraged acquisition and competitiveness, and men remained alienated from their own labor as well as from their fellow men. Social property had to replace private ownership as a prerequisite for moving from barbarism to civilization. But social ownership was *only* a prerequisite for creating a free society; if used incorrectly, it too could lead to new forms of tyranny. The individual and the flowering of his personality, unfettered by economic dictates, was the aim of structural rearrangement. The goal of socialist revolution was a system that would allow freely associating individuals to develop their own destinies. Social ownership was not an end in and of itself. "When the bread and butter problem is solved," Debs wrote in 1908, "and all men and women and children the world round are rendered secure from dread of war and fear of want, then the mind and soul will be free to develop as they never were before. We shall have a literature and an art such as the troubled heart and brain of man never before conceived. . . . We shall have beautiful thoughts and sentiments, and a divinity in religion, such as men weighted down by the machine could never have imagined."

Debs, unlike the more vulgar Marxists, maintained a vision of the future society. The struggle was for a distinct purpose, to move towards the liberation of mankind from all forms of oppression. "I am for socialism," Debs had stated in 1897, "because I am for humanity." Debs never lost sight of the goal for which the socialist movement was created. The inhumanities of an oppressive capitalism only led him to a renewed dedication to work for a condition of liberation.

Debs understood that to change America, he had to function as a revolutionary. The establishment of socialism depended upon the working class becoming politically conscious and moving outside the political framework developed by the bourgeois parties. The issues emphasized by the Republican and Democratic parties were only debates over tactical differences. Both, Debs argued, were dedicated to the continuation of the wage system—the very system that bred oppression, exploitation of labor, and war. His oath was not to politics in the bourgeois sense, but as he put it, "to the Blood-Red Banner of the Revolution." Political organization was the means by which the working class would attain conciousness and begin to effect a transformation of the system.

Politics to Debs meant that the revolutionary had to disavow the very purpose for which parties existed in capitalist society. Political campaigns were a means to talk to the working classes about the roots of their oppressive condition, a method to develop the conciousness that would give workers the power needed to move towards socialism. Even so, the danger existed that campaigns and elections would lead even the most committed socialist to define success in terms of votes cast and candidates elected. To Debs, this meant that the socialists might end up drifting in the direction of "bourgeois reform." The Socialist party was to Debs a "revolutionary party of the working class," and it opposed "vote-seeking for the sake of votes" and "office-seeking for the sake of office." The workers required an industrial union movement pledged to waging a class struggle. Only then would they express their economic solidarity by a political vote for the Socialist ticket. A vote cast for the Socialists would then be a vote *for* socialism, not a vote of individuals who backed the ticket in hopes of pressuring the Establishment for certain desired reforms.

Debs was to run for president on the Socialist line five different times: in 1900, 1904, 1908, 1912, and 1920. Ironically, his immense popularity throughout the nation and the large number of votes the party received when he was standard-bearer were as much a tribute to Debs as they were to socialism. The high point of socialist electoral strength came in 1912. Debs then polled 6 percent of the total presidential vote. Party members also held the greatest number of public offices in that year: 1,200 in 340 municipalities from coast to coast, including 79 mayorships in 24 states. Indeed, having gained these positions during a national contest against Progressive candidate Theodore Roosevelt, it appeared to many that the socialist votes were votes favoring social revolution, not reform.

Four years later, however, the socialist presidential vote declined from 897,000 to 590,000, and the percentage drop was even sharper. Debs's decision not to run in 1916 undoubtedly was part of the reason for the decline in the socialist vote, but this truth inadvertently testified to Debs's larger failure—a failure to create a mass socialist conciousness among all the members of his own constituency. In 1916 the socialists ran a virtual unknown, Allen L. Benson. While Debs had run ahead of the party ticket in 1912, Benson ran behind it in almost every state. The socialist vote increased after the entrance of the United States into World War I, but this was as much an antiwar vote as it was a vote for socialism. With renewed government repression of radicals, combined with massive doses of corporation-inspired social reforms, the Socialist party proved unable to challenge the more developed ways of the corporate capitalist system.

Another significant area of Debs's activity was his lifetime work among organized labor. Debs was instrumental in waging a fight against AFL craft unionism. Recognizing the avowedly conservative policies of the machine run by AFL chieftain Samuel Gompers, Debs never could understand the view of those socialists who argued that they should work within the AFL in an effort to transform it. By 1905, Debs hoped that the working classes would organize within the new Industrial Workers of the World. Here was a revolutionary union that organized workers on an industrial basis and that could function as an economic arm corresponding to the worker's political arm, the Socialist party. But IWW reliance on direct action and neosyndicalism and their disdain of the ballot soon led Debs to desert their ranks. He accomplished this not by open public disclosure and condemnation, but by quietly letting his membership lapse and by ceasing to speak on behalf of the IWW. Yet, when the Wobblies gained new strength by organizing unskilled immigrants during World War I, Debs sprang to their defense against Federal repression. Any enemy of the ruling class, he stated, was an ally of the oppressed.

When the war broke out, Debs remained true to his old ideal of international proletarian solidarity. At a time when many of the leading European socialist parties voted war credits for their own governments, Debs backed up the position of the Emergency Convention of the Socialist party. Their plea for militant antiwar action meant that those remaining in the party would face isolation at home and attack from defenders of the status quo. It meant in particular that anyone taking such a position would have to consider seriously the possibility of a long jail term as the price for adhering to his beliefs.

The war effort destroyed the fabric of American civil liberties during the Wilsonian era. Two months after the declaration of war, Congress approved conscription, the establishment of an official propaganda agency, and a law for the suppression of opposition and dissent. The Espionage Act of June 15, 1917, resulted in the first violations of the Constitution. The act prohibited criticism of the armed forces and interference with recruitment of troops. This section of the act provided the basis for prosecution of antiwar radicals who spoke out against official government policy. Radical newspapers such as *The Masses* and Victor Berger's *Milwaukee Leader* were deprived of second-class mailing privileges by order of the postmaster general. Statements opposing the war were termed violations of the act, because they could be construed to encourage disaffection in the armed forces. Free expression of ideas not hitherto subject to prosecution were now declared to be criminal acts. World War I created the first "ideological criminals" in the United States.

The Espionage Act was superseded on May 16, 1918, by the Sedition Act. This law, in effect, made *any* criticism of the government during wartime a criminal offense. Rose Pastor Stokes, who shifted sides as the war progressed and rejoined the antiwar socialists, was arrested for stating: "I am for the people, and the government is for the profiteers." The most famous victim of the Espionage Act was Debs, and his case was destined to become the most crucial of the free-speech, antiwar cases. Debs was arrested one month after the law was passed. His offense was to give a speech in Canton, Ohio, in which he questioned the talk about patriotic duty presented by some capitalists.

"It is not their but your duty that they are concerned about," Debs had stated, "their patriotic duty never takes them to the fire line or chucks them into the trenches." At his trial Debs made it clear that he was not appealing to the jury, but to popular opinion outside the court, particularly to the working class and the constituency of the antiwar movement. He used the courtroom and the trial in a political fashion, as a means of educating the populace to see where power resided in America. He refused to call witnesses and insisted on pleading his own case. Debs understood that in terms of the act itself, he indeed *was* guilty. His job was to reveal why a patently unconstitutional act had been passed by Congress, and why it was being used against the opponents of the war. He chose to make his defense on the sole basis of the First Amendment rights guaranteed by the United States Constitution. "That is the right I exercised at Canton," Debs proclaimed. "I believe in the right of free speech, in war as well as in peace." The war ended before his case reached the Supreme Court. Nevertheless, the Court upheld his sentence of ten years imprisonment on March 10, 1919, in a decision written by Justice Oliver Wendell Holmes.

The truth was, as Arthur A. Ekirch, Jr., has written, that American liberalism "had never before been so systematically undermined or suppressed as it was through the official action of the United States government during the second Wilson administration." At the war's end, the "illiberalism that followed the Armistice was worse than that of the war period." Socialists, radicals, conscientious objectors, and political prisoners were kept in prison. Wilson showed extreme vindictiveness towards Debs. He refused all pleas to issue a presidential pardon, although the socialists launched a massive clemency campaign that drew wide popular support. Debs was released only after Republican President Warren G. Harding was elected. Wilson, as one of the documents in this book reveals, viewed Debs as a traitor who was not to be forgiven. Ironically, the conservative Harding released Debs and then met with him at the White House. "We understand each other perfectly," Debs said of the new president. A free man, Debs was once again ready to attempt the job of building a socialist movement in America.

Debs reaffirmed his loyalty to the one battle he vowed he was willing to fight—the struggle for a world-wide proletarian revolution. But now the American socialist movement had been split apart. The Russian Bolsheviks had demanded that those in sympathy with them accept affiliation with the Third Communist International, and many of the younger new Left had broken with the Socialist party and joined the Communists.

Debs refused to acquiesce in the anticommunism displayed by many of his own comrades. Although he was anti-Communist Party, Debs continued to support and plead for understanding of the Bolshevik Revolution. Like others in his own party, Debs argued that "if you were to commit the [Socialist] party in America to the International program laid down by Lenin, you would kill the party." The "angry wrangling over the Moscow program," Debs noted, "was disrupting parties everywhere. . . . We must not enter a policy that means disruption." Yet Debs still felt that he was "heart and soul with our Russian comrades and the Soviet Republic." Lenin and Trotsky were called "colossal figures" whose "marvelous achievements" had "struck terror to the ruling class and inspired the workers of the world."

Debs therefore supported the Bolshevik Revolution, but at the same time favored an independent course of development for the American socialist movement. Because of Debs's immense popularity, all of the various Marxist groups tried to claim him as their own. The Communists overlooked Debs's critique of their party and invoked his name because Debs had defended the Soviet Revolution. The Socialists, who gradually became total anticommunists, pointed to Debs as premature anticommunist, citing Debs's opposition to the American Communist party. Both groups missed the point. Debs had stood with those who sought to fashion an independent American socialist movement, but he wanted that movement to be true to international proletarian solidarity. This meant a critical defense of the Soviet Revolution. It also meant that American socialists would have to develop their own program for revolution in the United States.

So it is with the theme of revolution that one must end. Debs has to be judged not by whether he was true to his own ideals, but by his everlasting commitment to building a socialist movement that would end private appropriation of property and allow for the development of a free society. It was his effort on this behalf that gave Debs his great nobility, and it is for this effort that he would have wished to be remembered.

Chronology of the Life of Debs

1855   Born November 5 to Jean Daniel and Marguerite Marie Debs in Terre Haute, Indiana.

1870   Leaves school and takes job in railroad enginehouse.

1872   Becomes locomotive fireman.

1875   Local of Brotherhood of Locomotive Firemen organized in Terre Haute; Debs becomes secretary of local.

1878   Becomes associate editor of the *Firemen's Magazine,* after Buffalo convention is held.

1880   Becomes grand secretary and treasurer of the Brotherhood of Locomotive Firemen and editor-in-chief of the union magazine.

1885   Marries Katherine Metzel of Pittsburgh.
Elected to one term in the Indiana legislature after running as a Democrat.

1892   Resigns offices in the Brotherhood, moving towards formation of a new railroad union.

1893   Organizes the American Railway Union, a new industrial union seeking to represent all railroad labor.

1894   ARU wins its first major struggle, an eighteen-day strike against James J. Hill's Great Northern Railroad.
George Pullman institutes harsh wage cuts against his laborers. Pullman workers ask ARU aid. Convention votes boycott on all Pullman cars, and work stoppages spread.
Federal court injunction prohibits ARU officers from helping strike. Debs arrested for conspiracy to obstruct delivery of federal mail, a violation of injunction. Grover Cleveland sends federal troops to Illinois.
Debs receives six months prison sentence for contempt of court and enters McHenry County Jail in Woodstock, Illinois.

1895   Studies socialism and meets with socialist leaders during his stay in prison. Meets Victor Berger, the Milwaukee Socialist, and reads Lawrence Gronlund's *The Co-Operative Commonwealth* and Edward Bellamy's *Looking Backward,* as well as the writings of the German Marxist, Karl Kautsky.

1896   Endorses William J. Bryan as the Democratic party candidate for president.

1897   Forms the Social Democratic party of the United States.

1900   Morris Hillquit leaves Daniel De Leon's Socialist Labor party, forming a separate branch of that group in Rochester, New York.

	Debs runs as presidential candidate of both the Social Democratic party and the Hillquit group, polling 100,000 votes.
1901	The Socialist party is created, based on a merger of the Hillquit "Rochester" group, Victor Berger's Milwaukee Socialists, and Deb's Social Democratic party.
1904	Debs runs as presidential candidate of the Socialist party, gaining a total vote of 400,000.
1905	Debs joins with William D. Haywood and other radicals to form the Industrial Workers of the World (IWW), a revolutionary syndicalist industrial union.
1906–7	Leads in the defense of William D. Haywood, Charles Moyer, and George Pettibone, who had been indicted for the bombing murder of former Governor Frank Steunenberg of Idaho. Jury finds them not guilty on August 2, 1907.
1908	Debs resigns from IWW because of tactical differences. Runs for office on presidential ticket of Socialist party, touring the nation in the chartered "Red Special" railroad train, polling 420,000 votes.
1912	Socialist party right and center pass amendment to party constitution banning advocacy of crime, sabotage, and other methods of violence. Debs runs for president on Socialist ticket, polling 900,000 votes, 6 percent of the total cast.
1917	Socialist party holds emergency convention in St. Louis, Missouri, on April 7, to formulate position on U.S. entrance into World War I. The party brands the congressional declaration of war "a crime against the people of the United States" and calls for strong opposition to the war and to conscription of U.S. troops.
1918	Speaking in Canton, Ohio, in June, Debs is indicted for violation of the Espionage Act. Brought to trial and sentenced to ten years in prison on September 14.
1920	Runs for president on the Socialist party ticket conducting his campaign from his prison cell; polls some 900,000 votes.
1921	Pardoned by executive order of the new Republican president, Warren G. Harding.
1922–23	Attempts to rebuild Socialist party, to work with other radicals including members of the new Communist organizations, and to chart a course for an American socialist movement.
1924	Supports Socialist party endorsement of Senator Robert M. LaFollette for president of the United States.
1926	Dies on October 20, 1926, at Lindlahr Sanitarium in northern Illinois.

DEBS LOOKS AT THE WORLD

1

Early Years with the American Railway Union: Debs as a Militant Union Leader

Debs's political education began with his experience as leader of the American Railway Union. Bolting from the craft-oriented Railroad Brotherhoods, Debs forged a militant industrial union that represented all railroad labor. Unlike the Brotherhoods, the ARU quickly became involved in strike activity against major roads. The most famous struggle was the strike against the Pullman Car Company. The strike against Pullman resulted in a Federal court injunction prohibiting strike activity, and led to Debs's arrest for violation of the court injunction. The following document, addressed to ARU members after Debs's jail sentence had been affirmed by the Supreme Court, indicates how Debs believed that the defeat suffered by the ARU had taught the railroad workers invaluable lessons for the future.

PROCLAMATION TO AMERICAN RAILWAY UNION[1]

Terre Haute, Ind., June 1, 1895

Sirs and Brothers—A cruel wrong against our great order, perpetrated by Wm. A. Woods, United States Circuit Judge, has been approved by the United States Supreme Court, and from under its shadow I address this communication to you; but though prison walls frown upon myself and others whom you choose as officials, I assure you that neither despondency nor despair has taken the place of the courage which has characterized our order since the storms of

---

[1] Issued when Debs's jail sentence for having participated in the Pullman strike was affirmed by the Supreme Court of the United States.

persecution first began to beat upon us. Hope has not deserted us. Our faith in the future of our great order is as strong as when our banners waved triumphantly over the Great Northern from St. Paul to the coast. Our order is still the undaunted friend of the toiling masses and our battle-cry now, as ever is the emancipation of labor from degrading, starving, and enslaving conditions. We have not lost faith in the ultimate triumph of truth over perjury, of justice over wrong, however exalted may be the stations of those who perpetrate the outrages.

The Storm and the Battle

I need not remind you, comrades of the American Railway Union, that our order in the pursuit of the right was confronted with a storm of opposition such as never beat upon a labor organization in all time. Its brilliant victory on the Great Northern and its gallant championship of the unorganized employees of the Union Pacific had aroused the opposition of every railroad corporation in the land.

To crush the American Railway Union was the one tie that united them all in the bonds of vengeance; it solidified the enemies of labor into one great association, one organization which, by its fabulous wealth, enabled it to bring into action resources aggregating billions of money and every appliance that money could purchase. But in this supreme hour the American Railway Union, undaunted, put forth its efforts to rescue Pullman's famine-cursed wage slaves from the grasp of an employer as heartless as a stone, as remorseless as a savage and as unpitying as an incarnate fiend. The battle fought in the interest of starving men, women, and children stands forth in the history of Labor's struggles as the great "Pullman Strike." It was a battle on the part of the American Railway Union, fought for a cause as holy as ever aroused the courage of brave men; it was a battle in which upon one side were men thrice armed because their cause was just, but they fought against the combined power of corporations which by the use of money could debauch justice, and, by playing the part of incendiary, bring to their aid the military power of the government, and this solidified mass of venality, venom, and vengeance constituted the foe against which the American Railway Union fought Labor's greatest battle for humanity.

Rewards and Penalties

What has been your reward for your splendid courage and manifold sacrifices? Our enemies say they are summed up in the one word "defeat." They point to the battlefield and say: "Here is where the host of the American Railway Union went down before the confederated enemy of labor." They point to the spot where Miles' serried soldiery stood with drawn swords, tramping steeds and shotted guns to kill innocent men whose only crime was devotion to wretched men and women, the victims of Pullman's greed. They designate the places where the minions of a despotic judge, the thieves and thugs, taken from Chicago slums, transformed into deputy marshals and armed with clubs and pistols, went forth to murder indiscriminately and to arouse the vengeance of the people by incendiary fires, and they point to the General Managers' Association, the Nero of the occasion, whose pitiless enmity of labor would have glorified in widespread conflagration rather than permitted a strike in the interest of famishing men, women and children, to have succeeded; and such disasters, say the enemies of labor, are the rewards of the courage of the ARU men, a courage as invincible as was ever displayed by Spartans, and which makes Pullman's Labor Thermopylæ to live in history as long as the right has a defender in the ranks of American workingmen.

Brothers of the American Railway Union, even in defeat our rewards are grand beyond expression, rewards which come only to brave men, the consciousness of noble deeds performed in the holy cause of labor's emancipation. Cowards, the fawning, sycophantic poltroons of power, never knew the thrills of joy that reward the heroes of battles fought in the interest of the oppressed.

> Once to ev'ry man and nation comes a moment to decide,
> In the strife of Truth and Falsehood, for the good or evil side.

The American Railway Union did decide. It espoused the cause of justice. It furrowed the land deeper with its plows of Truth and Courage than had fallen to the lot of any other labor organization since time began, and the seeds of emancipation which it sowed are germinating and a new era is destined to dawn upon labor.

Truth it is that the "Sons of brutish Force and Darkness," who have "drenched the earth with blood," chuckle over their victories. They point to the blacklisted heroes of the American Railway Union, idle and poor, and count upon their surrender. Their hope is that our order will disband; that persecution, poverty, and prison will do the work. These glory-handed enemies of our order expect to put out our lodge fires, silence our battle cries, to force us to disrobe ourselves of courage and manhood, permit them to place their ironshod hoofs on our neck, and sink us to fathomless depths of degradation and make the American Railway Union the synonym of all things the most detestable. . . .

Stand by Your Order!

At this supreme juncture I call upon the members of the American Railway Union to stand by their order. In God's own good time we will make the despot's prison, where innocent men suffer, monumental. We will link them with the legends and lore of labor's struggles to be read by our children and our children's children when Bartholdi's goddess of liberty with her torch enlightening the world has succumbed to the ravages of time.

> Count me o'er earth's chosen heroes—they were souls that stood alone.
> (While the men they agonized for threw the contumelious stone)
> Stood serene and down the future saw the golden beam incline
> To the side of perfect justice, mastered by their faith divine,
> By one man's plain truth to manhood and to God's supreme design.

2
Debs and American Socialism: The Early Years

Debs's imprisonment at Woodstock began the educational process that culminated in his adoption of the socialist perspective. The following three selections provide examples of what Debs meant by socialism, how he came to it, and why he described himself as a revolutionary. Rejecting the concern of Populists with "free silver," anti-imperialists with "expansion," Republicans with the gold standard, Debs stood unabashedly for an independent socialist politics, and he believed that the future was bright for its growth in the United States. The Progressivism of Theodore Roosevelt for Debs meant the repression of radical militants, and he rejected TR's "square deal" as phony. The option for him was "Revolution" and "Working Class Politics," a course he adhered to until his death in 1926.

HOW I BECAME A SOCIALIST [1]

As I have some doubt about the readers of *The Comrade* having any curiosity as to "how I became a Socialist" it may be in order to say that the subject is the editor's, not my own; and that what is here offered is at his bidding—my only concern being that he shall not have cause to wish that I had remained what I was instead of becoming a Socialist.

On the evening of February 27, 1875, the local lodge of the Brotherhood of Locomotive Firemen was organized at Terre Haute, Ind., by Joshua A. Leach, then grand master, and I was admitted as a charter member and at once chosen secretary. "Old Josh Leach," as he was affectionately called, a typical locomotive fireman of his day, was the founder of the brotherhood, and I was instantly attracted by his rugged honesty, simple manner, and homely speech. How well I remember feeling his large, rough hand on my shoulder, the kindly eye of an elder brother searching my own as he gently said, "My boy, you're a little young, but I believe you're in earnest and will make your mark in the brotherhood." Of course, I assured him that I would do my best. What he really thought at the time flattered my boyish

[1] *New York Comrade*, April, 1902.

vanity not a little when I heard of it. He was attending a meeting at St. Louis some months later, and in the course of his remarks said, "I put a tow-headed boy in the brotherhood at Terre Haute not long ago, and some day he will be at the head of it."

Twenty-seven years, to a day, have played their pranks with "Old Josh" and the rest of us. When last we met, not long ago, and I pressed his good right hand, I observed that he was crowned with the frost that never melts; and as I think of him now:

> Remembrance wakes, with all her busy train,
> Swells at my breast and turns the past to pain.

My first step was thus taken in organized labor and a new influence fired my ambition and changed the whole current of my career. I was filled with enthusiasm and my blood fairly leaped in my viens. Day and night I worked for the brotherhood. To see its watchfires glow and observe the increase of its sturdy members were the sunshine and shower of my life. To attend the "meeting" was my supreme joy, and for ten years I was not once absent when the faithful assembled.

At the convention held in Buffalo in 1878 I was chosen associate editor of the magazine, and in 1880 I became grand secretary and treasurer. With all the fire of youth I entered upon the crusade which seemed to fairly glitter with possibilities. For eighteen hours at a stretch I was glued to my desk reeling off the answers to my many correspondents. Day and night were one. Sleep was time wasted and often, when all oblivious of her presence in the still small hours my mother's hand turned off the light, I went to bed under protest. Oh, what days! And what quenchless zeal and consuming vanity! All the firemen everywhere—and they were all the world—were straining:

> To catch the beat
> On my tramping feet.

My grip was always packed; and I was darting in all directions. To tramp through a railroad yard in the rain, snow, or sleet half the night, or till daybreak, to be ordered out of the roundhouse for being an "agitator," or put off a train, sometimes passenger, more often freight, while attempting to deadhead over the division, were all in the program and served to whet the appetite to conquer. One night in midwinter at Elmira, N.Y., a conductor on the Erie kindly dropped me off in a snowbank, and as I clambered to the top I ran into the arms of a policeman, who heard my story and on the spot became my friend.

I rode on the engines over mountain and plain, slept in the cabooses and bunks, and was fed from their pails by the swarthy stokers who still nestle close to my heart, and will until it is cold and still.

Through all these years I was nourished at Fountain Proletaire. I drank deeply of its waters and every particle of my tissue became saturated with the spirit of the working class. I had fired an engine and been stung by the exposure and hardship of the rail. I was with the boys in their weary watches, at the broken engine's side and often helped to bear their bruised and bleeding bodies back to wife and child again. How could I but feel the burden of their wrongs? How could the seed of agitation fail to take deep root in my heart?

And so I was spurred on in the work of organizing not the firemen merely, but the brakemen, switchmen, telegraphers, shopmen, track-hands, all of them in fact, and as I had now become known as an organizer, the calls came from all sides and there are but few trades I have not helped to organize and less still in whose strikes I have not at some time had a hand.

In 1894 the American Railway Union was organized and a braver body of men never fought the battle of the working class.

Up to this time I had heard but little of Socialism, knew practically nothing about the movement, and what little I did know was not calculated to impress me in its favor. I was bent on thorough and complete organization of the railroad men and ultimately the whole working class, and all my time and energy were given to that end. My supreme conviction was that if they were only organized in every branch of the service and all acted together in concert they could redress their wrongs and regulate the conditions of their employment. The stockholders of the corporation acted as one, why not the men? It was such a plain proposition—simply to follow the example set before their eyes by their masters—surely they could not fail to see it, act as one, and solve the problem.

It is usless to say that I had yet to learn the workings of the capitalist system, the resources of its masters, and the weakness of its slaves. Indeed, no shadow of a "system" fell athwart my pathway; no thought of ending wage-misery marred my plans. I was too deeply absorbed in perfecting wage-servitude and making it a "thing of beauty and a joy forever."

It all seems very strange to me now, taking a backward look, that my vision was so focalized on a single objective point that I utterly failed to see what now appears as clear as the noonday sun—so clear that I marvel that any workingman, however dull, uncomprehending, can resist it.

But perhaps it was better so. I was to be baptized in Socialism in the roar of conflict and I thank the gods for reserving to this fitful occasion the fiat, "Let there be light!"—the light that streams in steady radiance upon the broadway to the Socialist republic.

The skirmish lines of the ARU were well advanced. A series of small battles was fought and won without the loss of a man. A number of concessions was made by the corporations rather than risk an encounter. Then came the fight on the Great Northern, short, sharp, and decisive. The victory was complete—the only railroad strike of magnitude ever won by an organization in America.

Next followed the final shock—the Pullman strike—and the American Railway Union again won, clear and complete. The combined corporations were paralyzed and helpless. At this juncture there was delivered, from wholly unexpected quarters, a swift succession of blows that blinded me for an instant and then opened wide my eyes—and in the gleam of every bayonet and the flash of every rifle *the class struggle was revealed*. This was my first practical lesson in Socialism, though wholly unaware that it was called by that name.

An army of detectives, thugs, and murderers was equipped with badge and beer and bludgeon and turned loose; old hulks of cars were fired; the alarm bells tolled; the people were terrified; the most startling rumors were set afloat; the press volleyed and thundered and over all the wires sped the news that Chicago's white throat was in the clutch of a red mob; injunctions flew thick and fast, arrests followed, and our office and headquarters, the heart of the strike, was sacked, torn out, and nailed up by the "lawful" authorities of the federal government; and when in company with my loyal comrades I found myself in Cook County jail at Chicago with the whole press screaming conspiracy, treason, and murder, and by some fateful coincidence I was given the cell occupied just previous to his execution by the assassin of Mayor Carter Harrison, Sr., overlooking the spot, a few feet distant, where the anarchists were hanged a few years before, I had another exceedingly practical and impressive lesson in Socialism.

Acting upon the advice of friends we sought to employ John Harlan, son of the Supreme Justice, to assist in our defense—a defense memorable to me chiefly because of the skill and fidelity of our lawyers, among whom were the brilliant Clarence Darrow and the venerable Judge Lyman Trumbull, author of the thirteenth amendment to the constitution, abolishing slavery in the United States.

Mr. Harlan wanted to think of the matter overnight; and the next morning gravely informed us that he could not afford to be identified with the case, "for," said he, "you will be tried upon the same theory as were the anarchists, with probably the same result." That day, I remember, the jailer, by way of consolation, I suppose, showed us the blood-stained rope used at the last execution and explained in minutest detail, as he exhibited the gruesome relic just how the monstrous crime of lawful murder is committed.

But the tempest gradually subsided and with it the bloodthirstiness of the press and "public sentiment." We were not sentenced to the gallows, nor even to the penitentiary—though put on trial for conspiracy—for reasons that will make another story.

The Chicago jail sentences were followed by six months at Woodstock and it was here that Socialism gradually laid hold of me in its own irresistible fashion. Books and pamphlets and letters from Socialists came by every mail and I began to read and think and dissect the anatomy of the system in which workingmen, however organized, could be shattered and battered and splintered at a single stroke. The writings of Bellamy and Blatchford early appealed to me. The "Cooperative Commonwealth" of Gronlund also impressed me, but the writings of Kautsky were so clear and conclusive that I readily grasped, not merely his argument, but also caught the spirit of his Socialist utterance—and I thank him and all who helped me out of darkness into light.

It was at this time, when the first glimmerings of Socialism were beginning to penetrate, that Victor L. Berger—and I have loved him ever since—came to Woodstock, as if a providential instrument, and delivered the first impassioned message of Socialism I had ever heard —the very first to set the "wires humming in my system." As a souvenir of that visit there is in my library a volume of "Capital," by Karl Marx, inscribed with the compliments of Victor L. Berger, which I cherish as a token of priceless value.

The American Railway Union was defeated but not conquered —overwhelmed but not destroyed. It lives and pulsates in the Socialist movement, and its defeat but blazed the way to economic freedom and hastened the dawn of human brotherhood.

OUTLOOK FOR SOCIALISM IN THE UNITED STATES [2]

I never think of these despised and persecuted "foreign invaders" without a feeling of profound obligation, akin to reverence, for their noble work in laying the foundations deep and strong, under the most trying conditions, of the American movement. The ignorant mass, wholly incapable of grasping their splendid teachings or appreciating their lofty motives, reviled against them. The press inoculated the public sentiment with intolerance and malice which not infrequently found expression through the policeman's club when a few

[2] *International Socialist Review,* September, 1900.

of the pioneers gathered to engraft the class-conscious doctrine upon their inhospitable "freeborn" American fellow citizens.

Socialism was cunningly associated with "anarchy and bloodshed," and denounced as a "foul foreign importation" to pollute the fair, free soil of America, and every outrage to which the early agitators were subjected won the plaudits of the people. But they persevered in their task; they could not be silenced or suppressed. Slowly they increased in number and gradually the movement began to take root and spread over the country. The industrial conditions consequent upon the development of capitalist production were now making themselves felt and Socialism became a fixed and increasing factor in the economic and political affairs of the nation.

The same difficulties which other countries had experienced in the process of party organization have attended the development of the movement here, but these differences, which relate mainly to tactics and methods of propaganda, are bound to disappear as the friction of the jarring factions smoothens out the rough edges and adjusts them to a concrete body—a powerful section in the great international army of militant Socialism.

In the general elections of 1898 upwards of 91,000 votes were cast for the Socialist candidates in the United States, an increase in this "off year" of almost 200 percent over the general elections of two years previous, the presidential year of 1896. Since the congressional elections of 1898, and more particularly since the municipal and state elections following, which resulted in such signal victories in Massachusetts, two members of the legislature and a mayor, the first in America, being elected by decided majorities—since then Socialism has made rapid strides in all directions and the old politicians no longer reckon it as a negative quantity in making their forecasts and calculating their pluralities and majorities.

The subject has passed entirely beyond the domain of sneer and ridicule and now commands serious treatment. Of course, Socialism is violently denounced by the capitalist press and by all the brood of subsidized contributors to magazine literature, but this only confirms the view that the advance of Socialism is very properly recognized by the capitalist class as the one cloud upon the horizon which portends an end to the system in which they have waxed fat, insolent, and despotic through the exploitation of their countless wage-working slaves. . . .

The campaign this year will be unusually spectacular. The Republican party "points with pride" to the "prosperity" of the country, the beneficent results of the "gold standard," and the "war record" of the administration. The Democratic party declares that "imperialism" is the "paramount" issue, and that the country is certain to go to the "demnition bow-wows" if Democratic officeholders are not elected instead of the Republicans. . . .

Both these capitalist parties are fiercely opposed to trusts, though what they propose to do with them is not of sufficient importance to require even a hint in their platforms.

Needless is it for me to say to the thinking workingman that he has no choice between these two capitalist parties, that they are both pledged to the same system, and that whether the one or the other succeeds, he will still remain the wage-working slave he is today.

What but meaningless phrases are "imperialism," "expansion," "free silver," "gold standard," etc., to the wage-worker? The large capitalists represented by Mr. McKinley and the small capitalists represented by Mr. Bryan are interested in these "issues," but they do not concern the working class.

What the workingmen of the country are profoundly interested in is the private ownership of the means of production and distribution, the enslaving and degrading wage-system in which they toil for a pittance at the pleasure of their masters and are bludgeoned, jailed, or shot when they protest—this is the central, controlling, vital issue of the hour, and neither of the old party platforms has a word or even a hint about it.

As a rule, large capitalists are Republicans and small capitalists are Democrats, but workingmen must remember that they are all capitalists, and that the many small ones, like the fewer large ones, are all politically supporting their class interests, and this is always and everywhere the capitalist class.

Whether the means of production—that is to say, the land, mines, factories, machinery, etc.—are owned by a few large Republican capitalists, who organize a trust, or whether they be owned by a lot of small Democratic capitalists, who are opposed to the trust, is all the same to the working class. Let the capitalists, large and small, fight this out among themselves.

The working class must get rid of the whole brood of masters and exploiters, and put themselves in possession and control of the means of production, that they may have steady employment without consulting a capitalist employer, large or small, and that they may get the wealth their labor produces, all of it, and enjoy with their families the fruits of their industry in comfortable and happy homes, abundant and wholesome food, proper clothing, and all other things necessary to "life, liberty and the pursuit of happiness." It is therefore a question not of "reform," the mask of fraud, but of revolution. The capitalist system must be overthrown, class-rule abolished, and wage-slavery supplanted by cooperative industry.

We hear it frequently urged that the Democratic party is the "poor man's party," "the friend of labor." There is but one way to relieve poverty and to free labor, and that is by making common property of the tools of labor.

Is the Democratic party, which we are assured has "strong socialistic tendencies," in favor of collective ownership of the means of production? Is it opposed to the wage system, from which flows in a ceaseless stream the poverty, misery, and wretchedness of the children of toil? If the Democratic party is the "friend of labor" any more than the Republican party, why is its platform dumb in the presence of Cœur d'Alene? * It knows the truth about these shocking outrages —crimes upon workingmen, their wives and children, which would blacken the pages of Siberia—why does it not speak out?

What has the Democratic party to say about the "property and educational qualifications" in North Carolina and Louisiana, and the proposed general disfranchisement of the Negro race in the southern states?

The differences between the Republican and Democratic parties involve no issue, no principle in which the working class has any interest, and whether the spoils be distributed by Hanna and Platt or by Croker and Tammany Hall is all the same to it.

Between these parties Socialists have no choice, no preference. They are one in their opposition to Socialism, that is to say, the emancipation of the working class from wage-slavery, and every workingman who has intelligence enough to understand the interest of his class and the nature of the struggle in which it is involved, will once and for all time sever his relations with them both; and recognizing the class struggle which is being waged between producing workers and nonproducing capitalists, cast his lot with the class-conscious, revolutionary Socialist party, which is pledged to abolish the capitalist system, class-rule and wage-slavery—a party which does not compromise or fuse, but, preserving inviolate the principles which quickened it into life and now give it vitality and force, moves forward with dauntless determination to the goal of economic freedom.

The political trend is steadily toward Socialism. The old parties are held together only by the cohesive power of spoils, and in spite of this they are steadily disintegrating. Again and again they have been tried with the same results, and thousands upon thousands, awake to their duplicity, are deserting them and turning toward

* [From March to July, 1892, the Executive Miner's Union had waged a solid but peaceful strike on behalf of a union shop and minimum wages. On July 11 union members armed themselves and seized two mines. The action resulted in intervention by Federal troops, who arrested 600 miners, and the troops began to function as a union-busting tool of the local employers.]

Socialism as the only refuge and security. Republicans, Democrats, Populists, Prohibitionists, Single Taxers are having their eyes opened to the true nature of the struggle and they are beginning to

> Come as the winds come, when
> Forests are rended;
> Come as the waves come, when
> Navies are stranded.

For a time the Populist party had a mission, but it is practically ended. The Democratic party has "fused" it out of existence. The "middle-of-the-road" element will be sorely disappointed when the votes are counted, and they will probably never figure in another national campaign. Not many of them will go back to the old parties. Many of them have already come to Socialism, and the rest are sure to follow.

There is no longer any room for a Populist party, and progressive Populists realize it, and hence the "strongholds" of Populism are becoming the "hotbeds" of Socialism.

It is simply a question of capitalism or Socialism, of despotism or democracy, and they who are not wholly with us are wholly against us.

Another source of strength to Socialism, steadily increasing, is the trades-union movement. The spread of Socialist doctrine among the labor organizations of the country during the past year exceeds the most extravagant estimates. No one has had better opportunities than the writer to note the transition to Socialism among trades unionists, and the approaching election will abundantly verify it.

Promising, indeed, is the outlook for Socialism in the United States. The very contemplation of the prospect is a wellspring of inspiration.

Oh, that all the working class could and would use their eyes and see; their ears and hear; their brains and think. How soon this earth could be transformed and by the alchemy of social order made to blossom with beauty and joy.

No sane man can be satisfied with the present system. If a poor man is happy, said Victor Hugo, "he is the pickpocket of happiness. Only the rich and noble are happy by right. The rich man is he who, being young, has the rights of old age; being old, the lucky chances of youth; vicious, the respect of good people; a coward, the command of the stouthearted; doing nothing, the fruits of labor."

With pride and joy we watch each advancing step of our comrades in Socialism in all other lands. Our hearts are with them in their varying fortunes as the battle proceeds, and we applaud each telling blow delivered and cheer each victory achieved.

REVOLUTION [3]

This is the first and only International Labor Day. It belongs to the working class and is dedicated to the Revolution.

Today the slaves of all the world are taking a fresh breath in the long and weary march, pausing a moment to clear their lungs and shout for joy, celebrating in festal fellowship their coming Freedom.

All hail the Labor Day of May!

The day of the proletarian protest,

The day of stern resolve,

The day of noble aspiration.

Raise high this day the blood-red Standard of the Revolution!

The banner of the Workingman.

The flag, the only flag, of Freedom.

Slavery, even the most abject—dumb and despairing as it may seem—has yet its inspiration. Crushed it may be, but extinguished never. Chain the slave as you will, O Masters, brutalize him as you may, yet in his soul, though dead, he yearns for freedom still.

The great discovery the modern slaves have made is that they themselves their freedom must achieve. This is the secret of their solidarity, the heart of their hope, the inspiration that nerves them all with sinews of steel.

They are still in bondage, but no longer cower.

No longer grovel in the dust,

But stand erect like men.

Conscious of their growing power, the future holds out to them her outstretched hands.

As the slavery of the working class is international, so the movement for its emancipation.

The salutation of slave to slave this day is repeated in every human tongue as it goes ringing round the world.

The many millions are at last awakening. For countless ages they have suffered, drained to the dregs the bitter cup of misery and woe.

At last, at last the historic limitation has been reached, and soon a new sun will light the world.

Red is the life-tide of our common humanity and red our symbol of universal kinship.

[3] *New York Worker*, April 27, 1907.

Tyrants deny it, fear it, tremble with rage and terror when they behold it.

We reaffirm it and on this day pledge anew our fidelity—come life or death—to the blood-red Banner of the Revolution.

Socialist greetings this day to all our fellow workers! To the godlike souls in Russia marching grimly, sublimely into the jaws of hell with the Song of the Revolution in their death-rattle; to the Orient, the Occident, and all the Isles of the Sea!

VIVE LA REVOLUTION!

The most heroic word in all languages is REVOLUTION.

It thrills and vibrates, cheers and inspires. Tyrants and time-servers fear it, but the oppressed hail it with joy.

The throne trembles when this throbbing word is lisped, but to the hovel it is food for the famishing and hope for the victims of despair.

Let us glorify today the revolutions of the past and hail the Great Revolution yet to come before Emancipation shall make all the days of the year May Days of peace and plenty for the sons and daughters of toil.

It was with Revolution as his theme that Mark Twain's soul drank deep from the fount of inspiration. His immortality will rest at last upon this royal tribute to the French Revolution:

> The ever memorable and blessed revolution, which swept a thousand years of villainy away in one swift tidal wave of blood—one: a settlement of that hoary debt in the proportion of half a drop of blood for each hogshead of it that had been pressed by slow tortures out of that people in the weary stretch of ten centuries of wrong and shame and misery the like of which was not to be mated but in hell. There were two Reigns of Terror, if we would but remember it and consider it: the one wrought murder in hot passion, the other in heartless cold blood; the one lasted mere months, the other lasted a thousand years; the one inflicted death on ten thousand persons, the other upon a hundred millions; but our shudders are all for the horrors of the minor Terror, so to speak; whereas, what is the horror of swift death by the axe compared with lifelong death from hunger, cold, insult, cruelty, and heartbreak? What is swift death by lightning compared with death by slow fire at the stake? A city cemetery could contain the coffins filled by that brief Terror, which we have all been so diligently taught to shiver at and mourn over, but all France could hardly contain the coffins filled by that older and real Terror which none of us has been taught to see in its vastness or pity as it deserves.

WORKING-CLASS POLITICS [4]

We live in the capitalist system, so-called because it is dominated by the capitalist class. In this system the capitalists are the rulers and the workers the subjects. The capitalists are in a decided minority and yet they rule because of the ignorance of the working class.

So long as the workers are divided, economically and politically, they will remain in subjection, exploited of what they produce and treated with contempt by the parasites who live out of their labor.

The economic unity of the workers must first be effected before there can be any progress toward emancipation. The interests of the millions of wage workers are identical, regardless of nationality, creed, or sex, and if they will only open their eyes to this simple, self-evident fact, the greatest obstacle will have been overcome and the day of victory will draw near.

The primary need of the workers is industrial unity and by this I mean their organization in the industries in which they are employed as a whole instead of being separated into more or less impotent unions according to their crafts. Industrial unionism is the only effective means of economic organization and the quicker the workers realize this and unite within one compact body for the good of all, the sooner will they cease to be the victims of ward-heeling labor politicians and accomplish something of actual benefit to themselves and those dependent upon them. In Chicago where the labor grafters, posing as union leaders, have so long been permitted to thrive in their iniquity, there is especially urgent need of industrial unionism, and when this is fairly under way it will express itself politically in a class-conscious vote of and for the working class.

So long as the workers are content with conditions as they are, so long as they are satisfied to belong to a craft union under the leadership of those who are far more interested in drawing their own salaries and feathering their own nests with graft than in the welfare of their followers, so long, in a word, as the workers are meek and submissive followers, mere sheep, they will be fleeced, and no one will hold them in greater contempt than the very grafters and parasites who fatten out of their misery.

It is not Gompers, who banquets with Belmont and Carnegie, [or] Mitchell, who is paid and pampered by the plutocrats, who are going to unite the workers in their struggle for emancipation. The Civic Federation, which was organized by the master class and consists of plutocrats, politicians, and priests, in connivance with so-called labor leaders, who are used as decoys to give that body the outward appearance of representing both capital and labor, is the staunch supporter of trade unions and the implacable foe of industrial unionism and Socialism, and this in itself should be sufficient to convince every intelligent worker that the trade union under its present leadership and, as now used, is more beneficial to the capitalist class than it is to the workers, seeing that it is the means of keeping them disunited and pitted against each other, and as an inevitable result, in wage-slavery.

The workers themselves must take the initiative in uniting their forces for effective economic and political action; the leaders will never do it for them. They must no longer suffer themselves to be deceived by the specious arguments of their betrayers, who blatantly boast of their unionism that they may traffic in it and sell out the dupes who blindly follow them. I have very little use for labor leaders in general and none at all for the kind who feel their self-importance and are so impressed by their own wisdom that where they lead their dupes are expected to blindly follow without a question. Such "leaders" lead their victims to the shambles and deliver them over for a consideration and this is possible only among craft-divided wage-slaves who are kept apart for the very purpose that they may feel their economic helplessness and rely upon some "leader" to do something for them.

Economic unity will be speedily followed by political unity. The workers once united in one great industrial union will vote a united working-class ticket. Not only this, but only when they are so united can they fit themselves to take control of industry when the change comes from wage-slavery to economic freedom. It is precisely because it is the mission of industrial unionism to unite the workers in harmonious cooperation in the industries in which they are employed, and by their enlightened interdependence and self-imposed discipline prepare them for industrial mastery and self-control when the hour strikes, thereby backing up with their economic power the verdict they render at the ballot box, it is precisely because of this fact that every Socialist, every class-conscious worker should be an industrial unionist and strive by all the means at his command to unify the workers in the all-embracing bonds of industrial unionism.

The Socialist party is the party of the workers, organized to express in political terms their determination to break their fetters and rise to the dignity of free men. In this party the workers must unite and develop their political power to conquer and abolish the capitalist political state and clear the way for industrial and social democracy.

But the new order can never be established by mere votes alone. This must be the result of industrial development and intelligent economic and political organization, necessitating both the industrial union and the political party of the workers to achieve their emancipation.

In this work, to be successfully accomplished, woman must have an equal part with man. If the revolutionary movement of the workers stands for anything it stands for the absolute equality of the sexes and when this fact is fully realized and the working woman takes her place side by side with the working man all along the battlefront the great struggle will soon be crowned with victory.

3
Socialism and Unionism

The relationship between unionism and socialism was always tenuous. Should the socialists work within the craft-dominated American Federation of Labor, as so many of the socialists argued? Should they break with the AFL and work with the revolutionary syndicalist Industrial Workers of the World, as Debs himself advocated for a short time? Or should they build both unionism and the Socialist party as two independent but complementary arms of working-class struggle? While finally opting for the latter approach, Debs was nonetheless merciless in his criticism of those socialists who capitulated to what he attacked as the reactionary leadership of the AFL, the wing led by Samuel Gompers and his business-unionist associates. Even after he abandoned the IWW, Debs never gave up his belief that it was only industrial unionism that would give workers sufficient power to move towards socialism.

REVOLUTIONARY UNIONISM [1]

The unity of labor, economic and political, upon the basis of the class struggle, is at this time the supreme need of the working class. The prevailing lack of unity implies lack of class consciousness; that is to say, enlightened self-interest; and this can, must and will be overcome by revolutionary education and organization. Experience, long, painful, and dearly bought, has taught some of us that craft division is fatal to class unity. To accomplish its mission the working class must be united. They must act together; they must assert their combined power, and when they do this upon the basis of the class struggle, then and then only will they break the fetters of wage slavery.

We are engaged today in a class war; and why? For the simple reason that in the evolution of the capitalist system in which we live, society has been mainly divided into two economic classes— a small class of capitalists who own the tools with which work is done and wealth is produced, and a great mass of workers who are compelled to use those tools. Between these two classes there is an irrepressible economic conflict. Unfortunately for himself, the work-

[1] Speech at Chicago, November 25, 1905.

29

ingman does not yet understand the nature of this conflict, and for this reason has hitherto failed to accomplish any effective unity of his class.

It is true that workers in the various departments of industrial activity have organized trade unions. It is also true that in this capacity they have from time to time asserted such power as this form of organization has conferred upon them. It is equally true that mere craft unionism, no matter how well it may be organized, is in the present highly developed capitalist system utterly unable to successfully cope with the capitalist class. The old craft union has done its work and belongs to the past. Labor unionism, like everything else, must recognize and bow to the inexorable law of evolution.

The craft union says that the worker shall receive a fair day's pay for a fair day's work. What is a fair day's pay for a fair day's work? Ask the capitalist and he will give you his idea about it. Ask the worker and, if he is intelligent, he will tell you that a fair day's pay for a fair day's work is all the workingman produces.

While the craft unionist still talks about a fair day's pay for a fair day's work, implying that the economic interests of the capitalist and the worker can be harmonized upon a basis of equal justice to both, the Industrial Worker says, "I want all I produce by my labor."

If the worker is not entitled to all he produces, then what share is anybody else entitled to?

Does the worker today receive all he produces? Does he receive anything like a fair (?) share of the product of his labor? Will any trade unionist of the old school make any such claim, and if he is bold enough to make it, can he verify it?

The student of this question knows that, as a matter of fact, in the capitalist system in which we live today the worker who produces all wealth receives but enough of his product to keep him in working and producing order. His wage, in the aggregate, is fixed by his living necessities. It suffices, upon the average, to maintain him according to the prevailing standard of living and to enable him to reproduce himself in the form of labor power. He receives, as a matter of fact, but about 17 percent of what his labor produces. . . .

The evolution is not yet complete.

By virtue of his private ownership of the social tool—made and used by the cooperative labor of the working class—the employer has the economic power to appropriate to himself, as a capitalist, what is produced by the social labor of the working class. This accounts for the fact that the capitalist becomes fabulously rich, lives in a palace where there is music and singing and dancing, and where there is the luxury of all climes, while the workingmen who do the work and produce the wealth and endure the privations and make the sacrifices of health and limb and life, remain in a wretched state of poverty and dependence.

The exploiting capitalist is the economic master and the political ruler in capitalist society, and as such holds the exploited wage worker in utter contempt.

No master ever had any respect for his slave, and no slave ever had, or ever could have, any real love for his master. . . .

Alert, vigilant, argus-eyed as the capitalist dailies of Chicago are, there is not one of them that knows of this meeting of the Industrial Workers. But if this were a meeting of the American Federation of Labor and an old trade union leader were here, you would read tomorrow morning a full account of it and him in every capitalist paper in the city. There is a reason for this that explains itself.

The capitalist papers know that there is such an organization as the Industrial Workers, because they have lied about it. Just now they are ignoring it. Let me serve notice on them through you and the thousands of others who flock to our meetings everywhere, that they will reckon with the Industrial Workers before six months have rolled around.

There are those wage workers who feel their economic dependence, who know that the capitalist for whom they work is the owner of their job, and therefore the master of their fate, who are still vainly seeking by individual effort and through waning craft unions to harmonize the conflicting interests of the exploiting capitalist and the exploited wage slave. They are engaged in a vain and hopeless task. They are wasting time and energy worthy of a better cause. These interests never can and never will be harmonized permanently, and when they are adjusted even temporarily it is always at the expense of the working class.

It is no part of the mission of this revolutionary working-class union to conciliate the capitalist class. We are organized to fight that class, and we want that class to distinctly understand it. And they do understand it, and in time the working class will also understand it; and then the capitalist class will have reason to understand it better still. Their newspapers understand it so well even now that they have not a single favorable comment to make upon it. . . .

There was a time when the craft union expressed in terms of unionism the prevailing mode of industry. That was long ago when production was still mainly carried on by handicraftmen with hand tools; when one man worked for another to learn his trade that he might become its master. The various trades involved skill and cunning; considerable time was required to master them. This was in the early stages of the capitalist system. Even at that early day the antagonism between employer and employed found expression, although the employer was not at that time the capitalist as he is today. The men who followed these trades found it necessary in order to protect themselves in their trade interests to band together, form a union, so that they might act together in resisting the encroachments of the "boss." So the trade union came into existence. . . .

The pure and simple trade union, in seeking to preserve its autonomy, is forced into conflict with other trade unions by the unceasing operation of the laws of industrial evolution. How many of the skilled trades that were in operation half a century ago are still practiced? . . .

We insist that all the workers in the whole of any given plant shall belong to one and the same union.

This is the very thing the workers need and the capitalist who owns the establishment does not want. He believes in labor union-ism if it is the "right kind." And if it is the right kind for him it is the wrong kind for you. He is more than willing that his employees shall join the craft union. He has not the slightest objection. On the contrary, it is easily proven that capitalists are among the most active upholders of the old craft unions.

The capitalists are perfectly willing that you shall organize, as long as you don't do a thing against them; as long as you don't do a thing for yourselves. You cannot do a thing for yourselves without antagonizing them; and you don't antagonize them through your craft unions nearly as much as you buttress their interests and prolong their mastery. . . .

President Roosevelt would have you believe that there are no classes in the United States. He was made president by the votes of the working class. Did you ever know of his stopping overnight in the home of a workingman? Is it by mere chance that he is always sheltered beneath the hospitable roof of some plutocrat? Not long ago he made a visit here and he gave a committee representing the workers about fifteen minutes of his precious time, just time enough to rebuke them with the intimation that organized labor consisted of a set of lawbreakers, and then he gave fifteen hours to the pluto-crats of Chicago, being wined and dined by them to prove that there are no classes in the United States, and that you, horny-handed veteran, with your wage of $1.50 a day, with six children to support on that, are in the same class with John D. Rockefeller! Your mis-fortune is that you do not know you are in the same class. But on election day it dawns upon you and you prove it by voting the same ticket.

Since you have looked yourself over thoroughly, you realize by this time that, as a workingman, you have been supporting, through your craft unions and through your ballots, a social system that is the negation of your manhood.

The capitalist for whom you work doesn't have to go out and look for you; you have to look for him, and you belong to him just as completely as if he had a title to your body; as if you were his chattel slave.

He doesn't own you under the law, but he does under the fact.

Why? Because he owns the tool with which you work, and you have got to have access to that tool if you work; and if you want to live you have got to work. If you don't work you don't eat; and so, scourged by hunger pangs, you look about for that tool and you locate it, and you soon discover that between yourself, a workingman, and that tool that is an essential part of yourself in industry, there stands the capitalist who owns it. He is your boss; he owns your job, takes your product, and controls your destiny. Before you can touch that tool to earn a dime you must petition the owner of it to allow you to use it, in consideration of your giving to him all you produce with it, except just enough to keep you alive and in working order.

Observe that you are displaced by the surplus product of your own labor; that what you produce is of more value under capitalism than you who produce it; that the commodity which is the result of your labor is of greater value under capitalism than your own life. You consist of palpitating flesh; you have wants. You have necessities. You cannot satisfy them, and you suffer. But the product of your labor, the property of the capitalist, that is sacred; that must be protected at all hazards. After you have been displaced by the surplus product of your labor and you have been idle long enough, you become restive and you begin to speak out, and you become a menace. The unrest culminates in trouble. The capitalist presses a button and the police are called into action. Then the capitalist presses button No. 2 and injunctions are issued by the judges, the judicial allies and servants of the capitalist class. Then button No. 3 is pressed and the state troops fall into line; and if this is not sufficient button No. 4 is pressed and the regular soldiers come marching to the scene. That is what President Roosevelt meant when he said that back of the mayor is the governor, back of the governor, the president; or, to use his own words, back of the city, the state, and back of the state the nation—the capitalist nation.

If you have been working in a steel mill and you have made more steel than your master can sell, and you are locked out and get hungry, and the soldiers are called out, it is to protect the steel and shoot you who made the steel—to guard the men who steal the steel and kill the men who made it.

I am not asking you to withdraw from the craft unions simply because the Industrial Workers has been formed. I am asking you to think about these matters for yourselves. . . .

I have said and say again that no strike was ever lost; that it has always been worth all it cost. An essential part of a working-man's education is the defeats he encounters. The strikes he loses are after all the only ones he wins. I am heartily glad for myself that I lost the strike. It is the best thing that ever happened to me. I lost the strike of the past that I may win the strike of the future.

I am a discredited labor leader, but I have good staying qualities. The very moment the capitalist press credits me with being a wise labor leader, I will invite you to investigate me upon the charge of treason. I am discredited by the capitalist simply because I am true to his victim. I don't want his favors. I do not court his approbation. I would not have it. I can't afford it. If I had his respect it would be at the price of my own.

I don't care anything about what is called public opinion. I know precisely what that means. It is but the reflection of the interests of the capitalist class. As between the respect of the public and my own, I prefer my own; and I am going to keep it until I can have both.

When I pick up a capitalist newspaper and read a eulogy of some labor leader, I know that that leader has at least two afflictions; the one is mental weakness and the other is moral cowardice—and they go together. Put it down that when the capitalist who is exploiting you credits your leader with being safe and conservative and wise, that leader is not serving you. And if you take exception to that statement, just ask me to prove it.

The rank and file of all unions, barring their ignorance, are all right. The working class as a whole is all right. Many of them are misguided, and stand in the light of their own interest.

It is sometimes necessary that we offend you and even shock you, that you may understand that we are your friends and not your enemies. And if we are against your unions it is because we are for you. We know that you have paid your dues into them for years and that you are animated by a spirit of misdirected loyalty to those unions.

I can remember that it was not a very easy matter for me to give up the union in which I had spent my boyhood and all the years of my young manhood. I remember that I felt there was something in it in the nature of a sacrifice, and yet I had to make it in the interest of the larger duty that I owed myself and the working class.

Let me say to you, if you are a craft unionist, that infinitely greater than your loyalty to your craft is your loyalty to the working class as a whole. No craft union can fight this great battle successfully alone. The craft is a part, a part only, of the great body of the working class. And the time has come for this class, numerically overwhelmingly in the majority, to follow in one respect at least the example of its capitalist masters and unite as a whole.

In this barbarous competitive struggle in which we are engaged, the workers, the millions, are fighting each other to sell themselves into slavery; the middle class are fighting each other to get enough trade to keep soul and body together, and the professional class are fighting each other like savages for practice. And this is called civilization! What a mockery! What a sham! There is no real civilization in the capitalist system.

Today there is nothing so easily produced as wealth. The whole earth consists of raw materials; and in every breath of nature, in sunshine, and in shower, hidden everywhere, are the subtle forces that may, by the touch of the hand of labor, be set into operation to transmute these raw materials into wealth, the finished products, in all their multiplied forms and in opulent abundance for all. The merest child can press a button that will set in operation a forest of machinery and produce wealth enough for a community.

Whatever may be said of the ignorant, barbarous past, there is no excuse for poverty today. And yet it is the scourge of the race. It is the Nemesis of capitalist civilization. Ten millions, one-eighth of our whole population, are in a state of chronic poverty. Three millions of these have been sunk to unresisting pauperism. The whole working class is in a sadly dependent state, and even the most favored wage-worker is left suspended by a single thread. He does not know what hour a machine may be invented to make his trade useless, displace him and throw him into the increasing army of the unemployed. . . .

You can change this condition—not tomorrow, not next week, nor next year; but in the meantime the next thing to changing it is making up your mind that it shall be changed. That is what we Industrial Unionists have done. And so there has come to us a new state of mind, and in our hearts there is the joy of service and the serenity of triumph.

We are united and we cannot be disunited. We cannot be stampeded. We know that we are confronted by ten thousand difficulties. We know that all the powers of capitalism are to be arrayed against us. But were these obstacles multiplied by a million, it would simply have the effect of multiplying our determination by a million, to overcome them all. And so we are organizing and appealing to you.

The workingman today does not understand his industrial relation to his fellow workers. He has never been correlated with others in the same industry. He has mechanically done his part. He has simply been a cog, with little reference to, or knowledge of, the rest of the cogs. Now, we teach him to hold up his head and look over the whole mechanism. If he is employed in a certain plant, as an Industrial Unionist, his eyes are opened. He takes a survey of the entire productive mechanism, and he understands his part in it, and his relation to every other worker in that industry. The very instant he does that he is buoyed by a fresh hope and thrilled with a new aspiration. He becomes a larger man. He begins to feel like a collective son of toil.

Then he and his fellows study to fit themselves to take control of this productive mechanism when it shall be transferred from the idle capitalist to the workers to whom it rightfully belongs.

In every mill and every factory, every mine and every quarry, every railroad and every shop, everywhere, the workers, enlightened, understanding their self-interest, are correlating themselves in the industrial and economic mechanism. They are developing their industrial consciousness, their economic and political power; and when the revolution comes, they will be prepared to take possession and assume control of every industry. With the education they will have received in the Industrial Workers they will be drilled and disciplined, trained and fitted for Industrial Mastery and Social Freedom.

4

Socialist Tactics, the IWW, and Defense Against Repression

In his famous article on socialist tactics, Debs revealed his agreement with the right and center of the Socialist party, which in 1912 sponsored an amendment to the party constitution banning advocacy of crime, sabotage, and other methods of violence. William D. Haywood, the noted IWW leader, was recalled from his position on the Socialist party's National Executive Committee for violating the ban in 1913. Debs considered himself a revolutionary, but condemned what he termed "the tactics of anarchist individualists" and in its place advocated the power of class consciousness.

While he did not advocate terrorism, Debs did favor active self-defense by the working class when under attack, including the purchasing of arms to ward off attacks by the corporation's private militia. Despite long-standing disagreement with the IWW, Debs consistently defended them against the growing repression that was to all but destroy the organization during World War I. Viewing the attack on the IWW as an attack against all organized labor, Debs urged a unified defense movement to fight all federal suppression of radicals.

SOUND SOCIALIST TACTICS [1]

Socialists are practically all agreed as to the fundamental principles of their movement. But as to tactics there is wide variance among them. The matter of sound tactics, equally with the matter of sound principles, is of supreme importance. The disagreements and dissensions among Socialists relate almost wholly to tactics. The party splits which have occurred in the past have been due to [the] same cause, and if the party should ever divide again, which it is to be hoped it will not, it will be on the rock of tactics.

Revolutionary tactics must harmonize with revolutionary principles. We could better hope to succeed with reactionary principles and revo-

[1] *International Socialist Review,* February, 1912.

lutionary tactics than with revolutionary principles and reactionary tactics.

The matter of tactical differences should be approached with open mind and in the spirit of tolerance. The freest discussion should be allowed. We have every element in every shade of capitalist society in our party, and we are in for a lively time at the very best before we work out these differences and settle down to a policy of united and constructive work for Socialism instead of spending so much time and energy lampooning one another.

In the matter of tactics we cannot be guided by the precedents of other countries. We have to develop our own and they must be adapted to the American people and to American conditions. I am not sure that I have the right idea about tactics; I am sure only that I appreciate their importance, that I am open to correction, and that I am ready to change whenever I find myself wrong.

It seems to me there is too much rancor and too little toleration among us in the discussion of our differences. Too often the spirit of criticism is acrid and hypercritical. Personal animosities are engendered, but opinions remain unchanged. Let us waste as little as possible of our militant spirit upon one another. We shall need it all for our capitalist friends.

There has recently been some rather spirited discussion about a paragraph which appears in the pamphlet on "Industrial Socialism" by William D. Haywood and Frank Bohn. The paragraph follows:

> When the worker, either through experience or study of Socialism, comes to know this truth, he acts accordingly. *He retains absolutely no respect for the property "rights" of the profit-takers. He will use any weapon which will win his fight.* He knows that the present laws of property are made by and for the capitalists. *Therefore he does not hesitate to break them.*

The sentences which I have italicized provoked the controversy.

We have here a matter of tactics upon which a number of comrades of ability and prominence have sharply disagreed. For my own part I believe the paragraph to be entirely sound.

Certainly all Socialists, knowing how and to what end capitalist property "rights" are established, must hold such "rights" in contempt. In the *Manifesto* Marx says: "The Communist (Socialist) revolution is the most radical rupture with traditional property relations; no wonder that its development involves the most radical rupture with traditional ideas."

As a revolutionist I can have no respect for capitalist property laws, nor the least scruple about violating them. I hold all such laws to have been enacted through chicanery, fraud, and corruption, with the sole end in view of dispossessing, robbing, and enslaving the working class. But this does not imply that I propose making an individual law-breaker of myself and butting my head against the stone wall of existing property laws. That might be called force, but it would not be that. It would be mere weakness and folly.

If I had the force to overthrow these despotic laws I would use it without an instant's hesitation or delay, but I haven't got it, and so I am law-abiding under protest—not from scruple—and bide my time.

Here let me say that for the same reason I am opposed to sabotage and to "direct action." I have not a bit of use for the "propaganda of the deed." These are the tactics of anarchist individualists and not of Socialist collectivists. They were developed by and belong exclusively to our anarchist friends and accord perfectly with their philosophy. These and similar measures are reactionary, not revolutionary, and they invariably have a demoralizing effect upon the following of those who practice them. If I believed in the doctrine of violence and destruction as party policy; if I regarded the class struggle as guerrilla warfare, I would join the anarchists and practice as well as preach such tactics.

It is not because these tactics involve the use of force that I am opposed to them, but because they do not. The physical forcist is the victim of his own boomerang. The blow he strikes reacts upon himself and his followers. The force that implies power is utterly lacking, and it can never be developed by such tactics.

The foolish and misguided, zealots and fanatics, are quick to applaud and eager to employ such tactics, and the result is usually hurtful to themselves and to the cause they seek to advance.

There have been times in the past, and there are countries today where the frenzied deed of a glorious fanatic like old John Brown seems to have been inspired by Jehovah himself, but I am now dealing with the twentieth century and with the United States.

There may be, too, acute situations arising and grave emergencies occurring, with perhaps life at stake, when recourse to violence might be justified, but a great body of organized workers, such as the Socialist movement, cannot predicate its tactical procedure upon such exceptional instances.

But my chief objection to all these measures is that they do violence to the class psychology of the workers and cannot be successfully inculcated as mass doctrine. The very nature of these tactics adapts them to guerrilla warfare, to the bomb planter, the midnight assassin; and such warfare, in this country, at least, plays directly into the hands of the enemy.

Such tactics appeal to stealth and suspicion, and cannot make for solidarity. The very teaching of sneaking and surreptitious practices has a demoralizing effect and a tendency to place those who engage in them in the category of "Black Hand" agents, dynamiters, safe-blowers, holdup men, burglars, thieves, and pickpockets.

If sabotage and direct action, as I interpret them, were incorporated in the tactics of the Socialist party, it would at once be the signal for all the *agents provocateurs* and police spies in the country to join the party and get busy. Every solitary one of them would be a rabid "direct actionist," and every one would safely make his "getaway" and secure his reward, à la McPartland, when anything was "pulled off" by their dupes, leaving them with their necks in the nooses.

With the sanctioning of sabotage and similar practices the Socialist party would stand responsible for the deed of every spy or madman, the seeds of strife would be subtly sown in the ranks, mutual suspicion would be aroused, and the party would soon be torn into warring factions to the despair of the betrayed workers and the delight of their triumphant masters.

If sabotage or any other artifice of direct action could be successfully employed, it would be wholly unnecessary, as better results could be accomplished without it. To the extent that the working class has power based upon class consciousness, force is unnecessary; to the extent that power is lacking, force can only result in harm.

I am opposed to any tactics which involve stealth, secrecy, intrigue, and necessitate acts of individual violence for their execution.

The work of the Socialist movement must all be done out in the broad open light of day. Nothing can be done by stealth that can be of any advantage to it in this country.

The workers can be emancipated only by their own collective will, the power inherent in themselves as a class, and this collective will and conquering power can only be the result of education, enlightenment and self-imposed discipline.

Sound tactics are constructive, not destructive. The collective reason of the workers repels the idea of individual violence where they are free to assert themselves by lawful and peaceable means.

The American workers are law-abiding and no amount of sneering or derision will alter that fact. Direct action will never appeal to any considerable number of them while they have the ballot and the right of industrial and political organization.

Its tactics alone have prevented the growth of the Industrial Workers of the World. Its principles of industrial unionism are sound, but its tactics are not. Sabotage repels the American worker. He is ready for the industrial union, but he is opposed to the "propaganda of the deed," and as long as the IWW adheres to its present tactics and ig-nores political action, or treats it with contempt by advising the workers to "strike at the ballot box with an ax," they will regard it as an anarchist organization, and it will never be more than a small fraction of the labor movement.

The sound education of the workers and their thorough organization, both economic and political, on the basis of the class struggle, must precede their emancipation. Without such education and organization they can make no substantial progress, and they will be robbed of the fruits of any temporary victory they may achieve, as they have been through all the centuries of the past.

For one, I hope to see the Socialist party place itself squarely on record at the coming national convention against sabotage and every other form of violence and destructiveness suggested by what is known as "direct action."

It occurs to me that the Socialist party ought to have a standing committee on tactics. The art or science of proletarian party tactics might well enlist the serious consideration of our clearest thinkers and most practical propagandists.

To return for a moment to the paragraph above quoted from the pamphlet of Haywood and Bohn. I agree with them that in their fight against capitalism the workers have a right to use any weapon that will help them to win. It should not be necessary to say that this does not mean the blackjack, the dirk, the lead pipe or the sawed-off shotgun. The use of these weapons does not help the workers to win, but to lose, and it would be ridiculous to assume that they were in the minds of the authors when they penned that paragraph.

The sentence as it reads is sound. It speaks for itself and requires no apology. The workers will use any weapon which will help them *win* their fight.

The most powerful and the all-sufficient weapons are the industrial union and the Socialist party, and they are not going to commit suicide by discarding these and resorting to the slingshot, the dagger, and the dynamite bomb.

Another matter of party concern is the treatment of so-called "intellectuals" in the Socialist movement. Why the term "intellectual" should be one of reproach in the Socialist party is hard to understand, and yet there are many Socialists who sneer at a man of intellect as if he were an interloper and out of place among Socialists. For myself I am always glad to see a man of brains, of intellect, join the movement. If he comes to us in good faith he is a distinct acquisition and is entitled to all the consideration due to any other comrade.

To punish a man for having brains is rather an anomalous attitude for an educational movement. The Socialist party, above every other, should offer a premium on brains, intellectual capacity, and attract to itself all the mental forces that can be employed to build up the Socialist movement, that it may fulfill its emancipating mission.

Of course the Socialist movement is essentially a working-class movement, and I believe that as a rule party officials and representatives, and candidates for public office, should be chosen from the ranks of the workers. The intellectuals in office should be the exceptions, as they are in the rank and file.

There is sufficient ability among the workers for all official demands, and if there is not, it should be developed without further delay. It is their party, and why should it not be officered and represented by themselves?

An organization of intellectuals would not be officered and represented by wage-earners; neither should an organization of wage-earners be officered by intellectuals.

There is plenty of useful work for the intellectuals to do without holding office, and the more intellectual they are the greater can their service be to the movement. Lecturers, debaters, authors, writers, artists, cartoonists, statisticians, etc., are in demand without number, and the intellectuals can serve to far better advantage in those capacities than in official positions.

I believe, too, in rotation in office. I confess to a prejudice against officialism and a dread of bureaucracy. I am a thorough believer in the rank and file, and in *ruling* from the *bottom up* instead of *being ruled* from the *top down*. The natural tendency of officials is to become bosses. They come to imagine that they are indispensable and unconsciously shape their acts to keep themselves in office.

The officials of the Socialist party should be its servants, and all temptation to yield to the baleful influence of officialism should be removed by constitutional limitation of tenure.

There is a tendency in some states to keep the list of locals a solemn secret. The sheep have got to be protected against the wolves. No one must know what locals there are, or who its officials, for fear they may be corrupted by outside influences. This is an effective method for herding sheep, but not a good way to raise men. If the locals must be guarded against the wolves on the outside, then someone is required to guard them, and that someone is a boss, and it is the nature of the boss to be jealous of outside influences.

If our locals and the members who compose them need the protection of secrecy, they are lacking in the essential revolutionary fiber which can be developed only in the play of the elements surrounding them, and with all the avenues of education and information, and even of miseducation and misinformation, wide open for their reception. They have got to learn to distinguish between their friends and their enemies and between what is wise and what is otherwise and until the rank and file are so educated and enlightened their weakness will sooner or later deliver them as the prey of their enemies. . . .

I cannot close without appealing for both the industrial and political solidarity of the workers.

I thoroughly believe in economic as well as political organization, in the industrial union and in the Socialist party.

I am an industrial unionist because I am a Socialist and a Socialist because I am an industrial unionist.

I believe in making every effort within our power to promote industrial unionism among the workers and to have them all united in one economic organization. To accomplish this I would encourage industrial independent organization, especially among the millions who have not yet been organized at all, and I would also encourage the "boring from within" for all that can be accomplished by the industrial unionists in the craft unions.

I would have the Socialist party recognize the historic necessity and inevitability of industrial unionism, and the industrial union reciprocally recognize the Socialist party, and so declare in the respective preambles to their constitutions.

The Socialist party cannot be neutral on the union question. It is compelled to declare itself by the logic of evolution, and as a revolutionary party it cannot commit itself to the principles of reactionary unionism. Not only must the Socialist party declare itself in favor of economic unionism, but the kind of unionism which alone can complement the revolutionary action of the workers on the political field.

I am opposed under all circumstances to any party alliances or affiliations with reactionary trade unions and to compromising tactics of every kind and form, excepting alone in event of some extreme emergency. While the "game of politics," as it is understood and as it is played under capitalist rules, is as repugnant to me as it can possibly be to any one, I am a thorough believer in political organization and political action.

Political power is essential to the workers in their struggle, and they can never emancipate themselves without developing and exercising that power in the interests of their class.

It is not merely in a perfunctory way that I advocate political action, but as one who has faith in proletarian political power and in the efficacy of political propaganda as an educational force in the Socialist movement. I believe in a constructive political program and in electing all the class-conscious workers we can, especially as mayors, judges, sheriffs, and as members of the state legislatures and the national Congress.

The party is now growing rapidly, and we are meeting with some of the trials which are in store for us and which will not doubt subject us to the severest tests. We need to have these trials, which are simply the fires in which we have to be tempered for the work bfore us.

There will be all kinds of extremists to deal with, but we have nothing to fear from them. Let them all have their day. The great body of the comrades, the rank and file, will not be misled by false teachings or deflected from the true course.

We must put forth all our efforts to control our swelling ranks by the use of wise tactics and to assimilate the accessions to our membership by means of sound education and party discipline.

The new year has opened auspiciously for us, and we have never been in such splendid condition on the eve of a national campaign.

Let us all buckle on our armor and go forth determined to make this year mark an epoch in the social revolution of the United States.

THE GUNMEN AND THE MINERS [2]

The time has come for the United Mine Workers and the Western Federation of Miners to levy a special monthly assessment to create a GUNMEN DEFENSE FUND.

This fund should be sufficient to provide each member with the latest high-power rifle, the same as used by the corporation gunmen, and 500 rounds of cartridges.

In addition to this every district should purchase and equip and man enough Gatling and machine guns to match the equipment of Rockefeller's private army of assasins.

This suggestion is made advisedly and I hold myself responsible for every word of it.

If the corporations have the right to recruit and maintain private armies of thieves, thugs and exconvicts to murder striking workingmen, sack their homes, insult their wives, and roast their babes, then labor unions not only have the right but it is their solemn duty to arm themselves to resist these lawless attacks and defend their homes and loved ones.

To the miners especially do these words apply, and to them in particular is this message addressed.

Paint Creek, Calumet, and Ludlow are of recent occurrence.

You miners have been forced out on strike, and you have been made the victims of every conceivable method of persecution.

You have been robbed, insulted, and treated with contempt; you have seen your wives and babes murdered in cold blood before your eyes.

You have been thrown into foul dungeons where you have lain for months for daring to voice your protest against these cruel outrages, and many of you are now cold in death with the gaping bullet wounds

[2] *International Socialist Review,* September, 1914.

in your bodies to bear mute testimony to the efficacy of government by gunmen as set up in the mining camps by the master class during the last few years.

Under government by gunmen you are literally shorn of the last vestige of liberty and you have absolutely no protection under the law. When you go out on strike, your master has his court issue the injunction that strips you of your power to resist his injustice, and then has his private army of gunmen invade your camp, open fire on your habitations, and harass you and your families until the strike is broken and you are starved back into the pits on your master's terms. This has happened over and over again in all the mining states of this union.

Now the private army of gunmen which has been used to break your strikes is an absolutely lawless aggregation.

If you miners were to arm a gang of thugs and assassins with machine guns and repeating rifles and order them to march on the palatial residences of the Rockefellers, riddle them with bullets, and murder the inmates in cold blood, not sparing even the babes, if there happened to be any, how long would it be before your officials would be in jail and your unions throttled and put out of business by the law?

The Rockefellers have not one particle more lawful right to maintain a private army to murder you union men than you union men would have to maintain a private army to murder the Rockefellers.

And yet the law does not interfere with the Rockefellers when they set up government by gunmen, and have their private army of mankillers swoop down on a mining camp, turn loose their machine guns, kill without mercy, and leave death, agony, and desolation in their wake, and therefore it becomes your solemn duty to arm yourselves in defense of your homes and in driving out these invading assassins, and putting an end to government by gunmen in the United States.

In a word, the protection the government owes you and fails to provide, you are morally bound to provide for yourselves.

You have the unquestioned right, under the law, to defend your life and to protect the sanctity of your fireside. Failing in either, you are a coward and a craven and undeserving the name of man.

If a thief or thug attacks you or your wife or child and threatens to take your life, you have a lawful right to defend yourself and your loved ones, even to the extent of slaying the assailant. This right is quite as valid and unimpaired—in fact it is even more inviolate—if the attack is made by a dozen or a hundred, instead of only one.

Rockefeller's gunmen are simply murderers at large, and you have the same right to kill them when they attack you that you have to kill the burglar who breaks into your house at midnight or the highwayman who holds you up at the point of his pistol.

Rockefeller's hired assassins have no lawful right that you miners are bound to respect. They are professional man-killers, the lowest and vilest on earth. They hire out to break your strike, shoot up your home, and kill you, and you should have no more compunction in killing them than if they were so many mad dogs or rattlesnakes that menaced your homes and your community.

Recollect that in arming yourselves, as you are bound to do unless you are willing to be forced into abject slavery, you are safely within the spirit and letter of the law.

The Constitution of the United States guarantees to you the right to bear arms, as it does to every other citizen, but there is not a word in this instrument, nor in any United States statute, state law, or city ordinance, that authorizes the existence of a private army for purposes of cold-blooded murder and assassination.

"Mine guard" is simply a master class term for a working class assassin.

Let the United Mine Workers and the Western Federation of Miners take note that a private army of gunmen is simply a gang of outlaws and butchers and that

They have not a solitary right an honest workingman is bound to respect!

Let these unions and all other organized bodies of workers that are militant and not subservient to the masters declare war to the knife on these lawless and criminal hordes and swear relentless hostility to government by gunmen in the United States.

Murderers are no less murderers because they are hired by capitalists to kill workingmen than if they were hired by workingmen to kill capitalists.

Mine guards, so-called, are murderers pure and simple, and are to be dealt with accordingly. The fact that they are in uniform, as in Colorado, makes them even more loathsome and repulsive than the common reptilian breed.

A "mine guard" in the uniform of a state militiaman is a copperhead in the skin of a rattlesnake, and possibly only because an even deadlier serpent has wriggled his slimy way into the executive chair of the state.

It remains only to be said that we stand for peace, and that we are unalterably opposed to violence and bloodshed if by any possible means, short of absolute degradation and self-abasement, these can be prevented. We believe in law, the law that applies equally to all and is impartially administered, and we prefer reason infinitely to brute force.

But when the law fails, and in fact, becomes the bulwark of crime and oppression, then an appeal to force is not only morally justified, but becomes a patriotic duty.

The Declaration of Independence proclaims this truth in words that burn with the patriotic fervor the revolutionary fathers must have felt when they rose in revolt against the red-coated gunmen of King George and resolved to shoot king rule out of existence.

Wendell Phillips declared that it was the glory of honest men to trample bad laws underfoot with contempt, and it is equally their glory to protect themselves in their lawful rights when those who rule the law fail to give them such protection.

Let the unions, therefore, arm their members against the gunmen of the corporations, the gangs of criminals, cutthroats, women-ravishers and baby-burners that have absolutely no lawful right to existence!

Let organized labor, from one end of the country to the other, declare war on these privately licensed assassins, and let the slogan of every union man in the land be

Down with government by gunmen and assassination in the United States!

THE IWW BOGEY [3]

The morning paper I have just read contains an extended press dispatch from Washington, under screaming headlines, making the startling disclosure that a world-wide conspiracy to overthrow the existing social order has been unearthed by the secret service agents of the government. The basis of the conspiracy is reported to have been the discovery of some guns and ammunition in the hold of a Russian freighter just arrived at a Pacific port in charge of a Bolsheviki crew, from which it has been deduced that the guns must have been sent by the Russian revolutionists to the IWW of the United States in pursuance of a conspiracy of the Russian reds, the Sinn Fein leaders of Ireland, and the American IWW's to overthrow all the governments of the civilized world.

This is really too much!

We are not told how the Sinn Feiners happen to get in on this universal conspiracy, but as their name, like that of the Bolsheviki and the IWW, has great potency as a bogey to frighten the feeble-minded, the inventors of this wonderful cock-and-bull story may well be allowed this additional license to their perfervid imagination.

Everything that happens nowadays that the ruling classes do not like and everything that does not happen that they do like is laid at the door of the IWW. Its name is anathema wherever capitalism wields the lash and drains the veins of its exploited victims.

It is a wonderful compliment! Is the working class wise to its signifi-

[3] *International Socialist Review,* February, 1918.

cance? Unfortunately not or the leaders and moving spirits of this persecuted industrial organization would not now be in jail waiting month after month to be tried for criminal offenses charged against them which they never dreamed of committing.

I think I may claim to be fairly well informed as to the methods and tactics of the IWW—with some of which I am not at all in agreement—and I have no hesitancy in branding the sweeping criminal charges made against them since the war was declared as utterly false and malicious and without so much as a shadow of foundation in fact.

Repeatedly the sensational charge has been spread broadcast through the capitalist press that the IWW were in conspiracy to blow up the mills and factories in the East, to burn the crops and destroy the orchards in the West, poison the springs and wells in the North, paralyze the cotton and rice industries in the South, and spread ruin and desolation everywhere for the profit and glory of the crazy Teuton Kaiser and his atrocious Junker plunderbund and the overthrow of democracy and freedom in the United States.

Was a more stupendous lie or a more stupid one ever hatched in a human brain?

Look at the IWW and then at the government and the more than one hundred million people of the United States! Is the lie not apparent on the very face of this absurd and malicious charge? Would any but an idiot or madman ever dream of the slaughter and destruction of an entire nation by a comparative handful of its population? Would any but a fool be deceived by such glaringly self-evident lies and calumnies?

Oh, the ghastly joke of it all! And the stark tragedy, too, when one thinks of the many simple-minded people whose attitude of fierce hostility toward the IWW and its leaders is determined by these inspired fabrications!

Why should the IW, organized for the very purpose of destroying despotism and establishing democracy, go across seas to lend its aid to the most brutal autocracy on the face of the earth?

Ah, but the autocracy within our own borders know how to play upon the prejudice and credulity of the unthinking and turn them against the men who at the peril of their freedom and their very lives are battling for the liberation of the people!

It is from Wall Street, the money center of the American plutocracy, that the campaign of falsehood and slander against the IWW is directed; from there that the orders are issued to raid its national and state offices, jail its leaders, break up its meetings, and tar and feather and lacerate with whips and finally lynch and assassinate its speakers and organizers.

Wall Street mortally fears the IWW and its growing menace to capitalist autocracy and misrule. The very name of the IWW strikes terror to Wall Street's craven soul.

But Wall Street does not fear Sammy Gompers and the AF of L.

Every plutocrat, every profiteering pirate, every food vulture, every exploiter of labor, every robber and oppressor of the poor, every hog under a silk tile, every vampire in human form, will tell you that the AF of L under Gompers is a great and patriotic organization and that the IWW under Haywood is a gang of traitors in the pay of the bloody Kaiser.

Which of these, think you, Mr. Wage-Slave, is your friend and the friend of your class?

It is interesting to note that at the very time the plutocracy and its hirelings are charging the IWW with treason and cramming the jails with its members they are also driving union labor out into the desert to perish under armed vigilantes as at Bisbee and Bingham, while in the same hour their Supreme Court outlaws picketing and legalizes and protects strike-breaking as in the cases of the union miners in West Virginia and the southwestern states.

There is one thing in this situation that is clear to every union man, to every sympathizer with the working class, and every believer in justice and fair play, and that is that the hundreds of IWW's and Socialists now in jail are entitled to be fairly tried. Upon that question there can be no difference among decent men, whatever may be their attitude toward the union and its principles. The Socialist Party, through its national executive committee—to its supreme credit—has taken this position and in a ringing declaration and appeal has expressed its determination that the accused IWW leaders and members receive a fair trial and a square deal.

To this end money will be needed, all that can be raised, and as the Captain Kidd Kaiser and his pirate crew of Junkers have not yet come across with that cargo of gold covering the purchase price of the IWW, it becomes the duty of every one who is with us to forthwith send his contribution to the defense of our shamelessly persecuted comrades.

This is our fight! We of the working class are all vitally interested in the outcome.

The war within the war and beyond the war in which the IWW is fighting—the war of the workers of all countries against the exploiters of all countries—is our war, the war of humanity against its oppressors and despoilers, the holiest war ever waged since the race began.

Let there be no mistake. The guerrilla warfare of Wall Street is not against the IWW alone but against the labor movement in general except in so far as union labor suffers itself to be emasculated and crawls on its belly at the feet of its despotic masters.

A spineless and apologetic union bearing the official seal of the Civic Federation is the noblest specimen of working-class patriotism in the eyes of our Wall Street rulers.

Now is the time to meet the attack, to resist the assault, to turn the guns on the real conspirators. The inevitable reaction will swiftly follow and instead of smashing the revolutionary labor movement this dastardly conspiracy will prove the making of it.

Now is the time for the fighting union men of America to stand together. The situation is the grimmest that ever confronted the working class but every such crisis bears with it the golden opportunity to the workers to strike the decisive blow and to forge ahead to a higher level of life. To take advantage of this supreme opportunity and profit by it to the limit, the workers must be united and act together like a well-disciplined army.

Solidarity must be the watchword!

As we stand upon the threshold of the year 1918 let us resolve to make it the most luminous one in the annals of proletarian achievement.

Industrial unity and political unity, the revolutionary solidarity of the working class, will give us the power to conquer capitalism and emancipate the workers of the world.

5
Socialist Politics

In 1912, Debs was to amass 6 percent of the presidential vote, as Socialist party candidate for president. Yet he had made it clear that a valid socialist politics could not be undertaken for the purpose of vote-getting. The purpose of a campaign was to make socialists, not to gain office; and Debs feared that the party would drift in the direction of "bourgeois reform." Debs's acceptance speech illustrates how he intended to use the campaign as a vehicle to create socialist consciousness.

DANGER AHEAD [1]

The large increase in the Socialist vote in the late national and state elections is quite naturally hailed with elation and rejoicing by party members, but I feel prompted to remark in the light of some personal observations during the campaign, that it is not entirely a matter for jubilation. I am not given to pessimism, or captious criticism, and yet I cannot but feel that some of the votes placed to our credit this year were obtained by methods not consistent with the principles of a revolutionary party, and in the long run will do more harm than good.

I yield to no one in my desire to see the party grow and the vote increase, but in my zeal I do not lose sight of the fact that healthy growth and a substantial vote depend upon efficient organization, the self-education and self-discipline of the membership, and that where these are lacking, an inflated vote secured by compromising methods can only be hurtful to the movement.

The danger I see ahead is that the Socialist party at this stage, and under existing conditions, is apt to attract elements which it cannot assimilate, and that it may be either weighted down or torn asunder with internal strife, or that it may become permeated and corrupted with the spirit of bourgeois reform to an extent that will practically destroy its virility and efficiency as a revolutionary organization.

To my mind the working class character and the revolutionary integrity of the Socialist party are of first importance. All the votes of the people would do us no good if our party ceased to be a revolutionary party, or only incidentally so, while yielding more and more to the

[1] *International Socialist Review,* January, 1911.

pressure to modify the principles and program of the party for the sake of swelling the vote and hastening the day of its expected triumph.

It is precisely this policy and the alluring promise it holds out to new members with more zeal than knowledge of working-class economics that constitutes the danger we should guard against in preparing for the next campaign. The truth is that we have not a few members who regard vote-getting as of supreme importance, no matter by what method the votes may be secured, and this leads them to hold out inducements and make representations which are not at all compatible with the stern and uncompromising principles of a revolutionary party. They seek to make the Socialist propaganda so attractive—eliminating whatever may give offense to bourgeois sensibilities—that it serves as a bait for votes rather than as a means of education, and votes thus secured do not properly belong to us and do injustice to our party as well as to those who cast them.

These votes do not express Socialism and in the next ensuing election are quite as apt to be turned against us, and it is better that they be not cast for the Socialist party, registering a degree of progress the party is not entitled to and indicating a political position the party is unable to sustain.

Socialism is a matter of growth, of evolution, which can be advanced by wise methods, but never by obtaining for it a fictitious vote. We should seek only to register the actual vote of Socialism, no more and no less. In our propaganda we should state our principles clearly, speak the truth fearlessly, seeking neither to flatter nor to offend, but only to convince those who should be with us and win them to our cause through an intelligent understanding of its mission.

There is also a disposition on the part of some to join hands with reactionary trade unionists in local emergencies and in certain temporary situations to effect some specific purpose, which may or may not be in harmony with our revolutionary program. No possible good can come from any kind of political alliance, express or implied, with trade unions or the leaders of trade unions who are opposed to Socialism and only turn to it for use in some extremity, the fruit of their own reactionary policy.

Of course we want the support of trade unions, but only of those who believe in Socialism and are ready to vote and work with us for the overthrow of capitalism.

The American Federation of Labor, as an organization, with its Civic Federation to determine its attitude and control its course, is deadly hostile to the Socialist party and to any and every revolutionary movement of the working class. To kowtow to this organization and to join hands with its leaders to secure political favors can only result in compromising our principles and bringing disaster to the party.

Not for all the vote of the American Federation of Labor and its labor-dividing and corruption-breeding craft unions should we compromise one jot of our revolutionary principles; and if we do we shall be visited with the contempt we deserve by all real Socialists, who will scorn to remain in a party professing to be a revolutionary party of the working class while employing the crooked and disreputable methods of ward-heeling and politicians to attain their ends.

Of far greater importance than increasing the vote of the Socialist party is the economic organization of the working class. To the extent, and only to the extent, that the workers are organized and disciplined in their respective industries can the Socialist movement advance and the Socialist party hold what is registered by the ballot. The election of legislative and administrative officers, here and there, where the party is still in a crude state and the members economically unprepared and politically unfit to assume the responsibilities thrust upon them as the result of popular discontent, will inevitably bring trouble and set the party back, instead of advancing it, and while this is to be expected and is to an extent unavoidable, we should court no more of that kind of experience than is necessary to avoid a repetition of it. The Socialist party has already achieved some victories of this kind which proved to be defeats, crushing and humiliating, and from which the party has not even now, after many years, entirely recovered.

We have just so much Socialism that is stable and dependable, because securely grounded in economics, in discipline, and all else that expresses class-conscious solidarity, and this must be augmented steadily through economic and political organization, but no amount of mere votes can accomplish this in even the slightest degree.

Voting for Socialism is not Socialism any more than a menu is a meal.

Socialism must be organized, drilled, equipped and the place to begin is in the industries where the workers are employed. Their economic power has got to be developed through sufficient organization, or their political power, even if it could be developed, would but react upon them, thwart their plans, blast their hopes, and all but destroy them.

Such organization to be effective must be expressed in terms of industrial unionism. Each industry must be organized in its entirety, embracing all the workers, and all working together in the interest of all, in the true spirit of solidarity, thus laying the foundation and developing the superstructure of the new system within the old, from which it is evolving, and systematically fitting the workers, step by step, to assume entire control of the productive forces when the hour strikes for the impending organic change.

Without such economic organization and the economic power with which it is clothed, and without the industrial cooperative training, discipline, and efficiency which are its corollaries, the fruit of any political victories the workers may achieve will turn to ashes on their lips.

Now that the capitalist system is so palpably breaking down, and in consequence its political parties breaking up, the disintegrating elements with vague reform ideas and radical bourgeois tendencies will head in increasing numbers toward the Socialist party, especially since the greatly enlarged vote of this year has been announced and the party is looming up as a possible dispenser of the spoils of office. There is danger, I believe, that the party may be swamped by such an exodus and the best possible means, and in fact, the only effectual means of securing the party against such a fatality is the economic power of the industrially organized workers.

The votes will come rapidly enough from now on without seeking them and we should make it clear that the Socialist party wants the votes only of those who want Socialism, and that, above all, as a revolutionary party of the working class, it discountenances vote-seeking for the sake of votes and holds in contempt office-seeking for the sake of office. These belong entirely to capitalist parties with their bosses and their boodle and have no place in a party whose shibboleth is emancipation.

With the workers efficiently organized industrially, bound together by the common tie of their enlightened self-interest, they will just as naturally and inevitably express their economic solidarity in political terms and cast a united vote for the party of their class as the forces of nature express obedience to the laws of gravitation.

SPEECH OF ACCEPTANCE [2]

It is with a full sense of the responsibility it imposes and the service it exacts that I accept the nomination for president tendered to me by the Socialist party of the United States. Personally I did not wish the nomination. It came to me unsought. It came as summons to service and not as a personal honor.

Every true member of the Socialist party is at the party's service. The confidence of his comrades is to him a sacred trust and their collective will the party's law.

My chief concern as a presidential candidate is that I shall serve well the party, and the class and the cause the party represents.

[2] *International Socialist Review*, October, 1912.

Socialist Party Different

The Socialist party is fundamentally different from all other parties. It came in the process of evolution and grows with the growth of the forces which created it. Its spirit is militant and its aim revolutionary. It expresses in political terms the aspiration of the working class to freedom and to a larger and fuller life than they have yet known.

The world's workers have always been and still are the world's slaves. They have borne all the burdens of the race and built all the monuments along the track of civilization; they have produced all the world's wealth and supported all the world's governments. They have conquered all things but their own freedom. They are still the subject class in every nation on earth and the chief function of every government is to keep them at the mercy of their masters.

The workers in the mills and factories, in the mines and on the farms and railways never had a party of their own until the Socialist party was organized. They divided their votes between the parties of their masters. They did not realize that they were using their ballots to forge their own fetters.

But the awakening came. It was bound to come. Class rule became more and more oppressive and wage slavery more and more galling. The eyes of the workers began to open. They began to see the cause of the misery they had dumbly suffered so many years. It dawned upon them that society was divided into two classes—capitalists and workers, exploiters and producers; that the capitalists, while comparatively few, owned the nation and controlled the government; that the courts and the soldiers were at their command, and that the workers, while in a great majority, were in slavish subjection.

When they ventured to protest they were discharged and found themselves blacklisted; when they went out on strike they were suppressed by the soldiers and sent to jail.

They looked about them and saw a land of wonderful resources; they saw the productive machinery made by their own hands and the vast wealth produced by their own labor, in the shadow of which their wives and children were perishing in the skeleton clutch of famine.

Began to Think

The very suffering they were forced to endure quickened their senses. They began to think. A new light dawned upon their dark skies. They rubbed the age-long sleep from their eyes. They had long felt the brutalizing effect of class rule; now they saw the cause of it. Slowly but steadily they became class conscious. They said, "We are brothers, we are comrades," and they saw themselves multiplied by millions. They caught the prophetic battle cry of Karl Marx, the world's greatest labor leader, the inspired evangel of working-class emancipation, "Workers of all countries, unite!"

And now, behold! The international Socialist movement spreads out over all the nations of the earth. The world's workers are aroused at last. They are no longer on their knees; their bowed bodies are now erect. Despair has given way to hope, weakness to strength, fear to courage. They no longer cringe and supplicate; they hold up their heads and command. They have ceased to fear their masters and have learned to trust themselves.

And this is how the Socialist party came to be born. It was quickened into life in the bitter struggle of the world's enslaved workers. It expresses their collective determination to break their fetters and emancipate themselves and the race.

Is it strange that the workers are loyal to such a party, that they proudly stand beneath its blazing banners and fearlessly proclaim its conquering principles? It is the one party of their class, born of their agony and baptized in the blood of their countless brethren who perished in the struggle to give it birth.

Hail to this great party of the toiling millions whose battle cry is heard around the world!

Doesn't Plead for Votes

We do not plead for votes; the workers give them freely the hour they understand.

But we need to destroy the prejudice that still exists and dispel the darkness that still prevails in the working-class world. We need the clear light of sound education and the conquering power of economic and political organization.

Before the unified hosts of labor all the despotic governments on earth are powerless and all resistance vain. Before their onward march all ruling classes disappear and all slavery vanishes forever.

The appeal of the Socialist party is to all the useful people of the nation, all who work with brain and muscle to produce the nation's wealth and who promote its progress and conserve its civilization.

Only they who bear its burdens may rightfully enjoy the blessings of civilized society.

There are no boundary lines to separate race from race, sex from sex, or creed from creed in the Socialist party. The common rights of all are equally recognized.

Every human being is entitled to sunlight and air, to what his labor produces, and to an equal chance with every other human being to unfold and ripen and give to the world the riches of his mind and soul.

Economic slavery is the world's greatest curse today. Poverty and misery, prostitution, insanity, and crime are its inevitable results.

The Socialist party is the one party which stands squarely and uncompromisingly for the abolition of industrial slavery; the one party pledged in every fiber of its being to the economic freedom of all the people.

So long as the nation's resources and productive and distributive machinery are the private property of a privileged class the masses will be at their mercy, poverty will be their lot and life will be shorn of all that raises it above the brute level.

New Progressive Party

The infallible test of a political party is the private ownership of the sources of wealth and the means of life. Apply that test to the Republican, Democratic, and Progressive parties and upon that basic, fundamental issue you will find them essentially one and the same. They differ according to the conflicting interests of the privileged classes, but at bottom they are alike and stand for capitalist class rule and working-class slavery.

The new Progressive party is a party of progressive capitalism. It is lavishly financed and shrewdly advertised. But it stands for the rule of capitalism all the same.

When the owners of the trusts finance a party to put themselves out of business; when they turn over their wealth to the people from whom they stole it and go to work for a living, it will be time enough to consider the merits of the Roosevelt Progressive party.

One question is sufficient to determine the true status of all these parties. Do they want the workers to own the tools they work with, control their own jobs, and secure to themselves the wealth they produce? Certainly not. That is utterly ridiculous and impossible from their point of view.

The Republican, Democratic, and Progressive parties all stand for the private ownership by the capitalists of the productive machinery used by the workers, so that the capitalists can continue to filch the wealth produced by the workers.

The Socialist party is the only party which declares that the tools of labor belong to labor and that the wealth produced by the working class belongs to the working class.

Intelligent workingmen are no longer deceived. They know that the struggle in which the world is engaged today is a class struggle and that in this struggle the workers can never win by giving their votes to capitalist parties. They have tried this for many years and it has always produced the same result to them.

The class of privilege and pelf has had the world by the throat and the working class beneath its iron-shod hoofs long enough. The magic word of freedom is ringing through the nation and the spirit of intelligent revolt is finding expression in every land beneath the sun.

The solidarity of the working class is the salient force in the social transformation of which we behold the signs upon every hand. Nearer and nearer they are being drawn together in the bonds of unionism; clearer and clearer becomes their collective vision; greater and greater the power that throbs within them.

Hosts of Freedom

They are the twentieth-century hosts of freedom who are to destroy all despotisms, topple over all thrones, seize all sceptres of authority and hold them in their own strong hands, tear up all privilege by the roots, and consecrate the earth and all its fullness to the joy and service of all humanity.

It is vain to hope for material relief upon the prevailing system of capitalism. All the reforms that are proposed by the three capitalist parties, even if carried out in good faith, would still leave the working class in industrial slavery.

The working class will never be emancipated by the grace of the capitalists class, but only by overthrowing that class.

The power to emancipate itself is inherent in the working class, and this power must be developed through sound education and applied through sound organization.

It is as foolish and self-destructive for workingmen to turn to Republican, Democratic, and Progressive parties on election day as it would be for them to turn to the Manufacturers' Association and the Citizens' Alliance when they are striking against starvation wages.

The capitalist class is organized economically and politically to keep the working class in subjection and perpetuate its power as a ruling class. They do not support a working-class union nor a working-class party. They are not so foolish. They wisely look out for themselves.

The capitalist class despise a working-class party. Why should the working class give their support to a capitalist-class party?

Capitalist misrule under which workingmen suffer slavery and the most galling injustice exists only because it has workingmen's support. Withdraw that support and capitalism is dead.

The capitalists can enslave and rob the workers only by the consent of the workers when they cast their ballots on election day.

Every vote cast for a capitalist party, whatever its name, is a vote for wage-slavery, for poverty and degradation.

Every vote cast for the Socialist party, the workers' own party, is a vote for emancipation.

We appeal to the workers and to all who sympathize with them to make their power felt in this campaign. Never before has there been so great an opportunity to strike an effective blow for freedom.

Capitalism Doomed

Capitalism is rushing blindly to its impending doom. All the signs portend the inevitable breakdown of the existing order. Deep-seated discontent has seized upon the masses. They must indeed be deaf who do not hear the mutterings of the approaching storm.

Poverty, high prices, unemployment, child slavery, widespread misery and haggard want in a land bursting with abundance; prostitution and insanity, suicide and crime, these in solemn numbers tell the tragic story of capitalism's saturnalia of blood and tears and shame as its end draws near.

It is to abolish this monstrous system and the misery and crime which flow from it in a direful and threatening stream that the Socialist party was organized and now makes its appeal to the intelligence and conscience of the people. Social reorganization is the imperative demand of this world-wide revolutionary movement.

The Socialist party's emission is not only to destroy capitalist despotism but to establish industrial and social democracy. To this end the workers are steadily organizing and fitting themselves for the day when they shall take control of the people's industries and when the right to work shall be as inviolate as the right to breathe the breath of life.

Standing as it does for the emancipation of the working class from wage-slavery, for the equal rights and opportunities of all men and all women, for the abolition of child labor and the conservation of all childhood, for social self-rule and the equal freedom of all, the Socialist party is the party of progress, the party of the future, and its triumph will signalize the birth of a new civilization and the dawn of a happier day for all humanity.

6
Oppressed Minorities:
The Negro and the Woman

Within the Socialist party, a party that was contami-
nated with racism, Debs stood out as a forthright supporter of
Negro rights. Debs understood as early as 1903 that "the history
of the Negro in the United States is a history of crime without a
parallel." Yet he argued that the Negro question could be reduced
to a simple "labor question," and that concern with questions of
"social equality" was a subterfuge meant to hide the real issue,
"economic freedom."

Similarly, Debs attacked those who showed attitudes of male
superiority and who believed the woman had to be kept in sub-
jection. He sided with the feminist movement and the suffragettes,
standing far ahead of his own time.

THE NEGRO IN THE CLASS STRUGGLE [1]

It so happens that I write upon the Negro question, in compliance
with the request of the editor of the *International Socialist Review,* in
the state of Louisiana, where the race prejudice is as strong and the
feeling against the "nigger" as bitter and relentless as when Lincoln's
proclamation of emancipation lashed the waning Confederacy into
fury and incited the final and desperate attempts to burst the bonds
that held the southern states in the federal union. Indeed, so thoroughly is the South permeated with the malign spirit of race hatred
that even Socialists are to be found, and by no means rarely, who either
share directly in the race hostility against the Negro, or avoid the issue,
or apologize for the social obliteration of the color line in the class
struggle.

The white man in the South declares that "the nigger is all right in
his place"; that is, as menial, servant, and slave. If he dare hold up his
head, feel the thrill of manhood in his veins, and nurse the hope that
some day may bring deliverance; if in his brain the thought of freedom
dawns and in his heart the aspiration to rise above the animal plane
and propensities of his sires, he must be made to realize that notwith-

standing the white man is civilized (?) the black man is a "nigger" still and must so remain as long as planets wheel in space.

But while the white man is considerate enough to tolerate the Negro "in his place," the remotest suggestion at social recognition arouses all the pent-up wrath of his Anglo-Saxon civilization; and my observation is that the less real ground there is for such indignant assertion of self-superiority, the more passionately it is proclaimed.

At Yoakum, Texas, a few days ago, leaving the depot with two grips in my hands, I passed four or five bearers of the white man's burden perched on a railing and decorating their environment with tobacco juice. One of them, addressing me, said: "There's a nigger that'll carry your grips." A second one added: "That's what he's here for," and the third chimed in with: "That's right, by God." Here was a savory bouquet of white superiority. One glance was sufficient to satisfy me that they represented all there is of justification for the implacable hatred of the Negro race. They were ignorant, lazy, unclean, totally void of ambition, themselves the foul product of the capitalist system and held in lowest contempt by the master class, yet esteeming themselves immeasurably above the cleanest, most intelligent, and self-respecting Negro, having by reflex absorbed the "nigger" hatred of their masters.

As a matter of fact the industrial supremacy of the South before the war would not have been possible without the Negro, and the South of today would totally collapse without his labor. Cotton culture has been and is the great staple and it will not be denied that the fineness and superiority of the fiber that makes the export of the Southern states the greatest in the world is due in large measure to the genius of the Negroes charged with its cultivation.

The whole world is under obligation to the Negro, and that the white heel is still upon the black neck is simply proof that the world is not yet civilized.

The history of the Negro in the United States is a history of crime without a parallel.

Why should the white man hate him? Because he stole him from his native land and for two centuries and a half robbed him of the fruit of his labor, kept him in beastly ignorance, and subjected him to the brutal domination of the lash? Because he tore the black child from the breasts of its mother and ravished the black man's daughter before her father's eyes?

There are thousands of Negroes who bear testimony in their whitening skins that men who so furiously resent the suggestion of "social equality" are far less sensitive in respect to the sexual equality of the races.

But of all the senseless agitation in capitalist society, that in respect to "social equality" takes the palm. The very instant it is mentioned the old aristocratic plantation owner's shrill cry about the "buck nigger" marrying the "fair young daughter" of his master is heard from the tomb and echoed and re-echoed across the spaces and repeated by the "white trash" in proud vindication of their social superiority.

Social equality, forsooth! Is the black man pressing his claims for social recognition upon his white burden-bearer? Is there any reason why he should? Is the white man's social recognition of his own white brother such as to excite the Negro's ambition to covet the noble prize? Has the Negro any greater desire, or is there any reason why he should have, for social intercourse with the white man than the white man has for social relations with the Negro? This phase of the Negro question is pure fraud and serves to mask the real issue, which is not *social equality,* but *economic freedom.*

There never was any social inferiority that was not the shrivelled fruit of economic inequality.

The Negro, given economic freedom, will not ask the white man any social favors; and the burning question of "social equality" will disappear like mist before the sunrise.

I have said and say again that, properly speaking, there is no Negro question outside of the labor question—the working-class struggle. Our position as Socialists and as a party is perfectly plain. We have simply to say: "The class struggle is colorless." The capitalists, white, black, and other shades, are on one side and the workers, white, black, and all other colors, on the other side.

When Marx said: "Workingmen of all countries unite," he gave concrete expression to the socialist philosophy of the class struggle; unlike the framers of the Declaration of Independence who announced that "all men are created equal" and then basely repudiated their own doctrine, Marx issued the call to all the workers of the globe, regardless of race, sex, creed, or any other condition whatsoever.

As a social party we receive the Negro and all other races upon absolutely equal terms. We are the party of the working class, the whole working class, and we will not suffer ourselves to be divided by any specious appeal to race prejudice; and if we should be coaxed or driven from the straight road we will be lost in the wilderness and ought to perish there, for we shall no longer be a Socialist party.

Let the capitalist press and capitalist "public opinion" indulge themselves in alternate flattery and abuse of the Negro; we as Socialists will receive him in our party, treat him in our counsels, and stand by him all around the same as if his skin were white instead of black; and this we do, not from any considerations of sentiment, but because it accords with the philosophy of Socialism, the genius of the class struggle, and is eternally right and bound to triumph in the end.

With the "nigger" question, the "race war" from the capitalist view-point we have nothing to do. In capitalism the Negro question is a grave one and will grow more threatening as the contradictions and complications of capitalist society multiply, but this need not worry us. Let them settle the Negro question in their way, if they can. We have nothing to do with it, for that is their fight. We have simply to open the eyes of as many Negroes as we can and bring them into the Socialist movement to do battle for emancipation from wage-slavery, and when the working class have triumphed in the class struggle and stand forth economic as well as political free men, the race problem will forever disappear.

Socialists should with pride proclaim their sympathy with and fealty to the black race, and if any there be who hesitate to avow themselves in the face of ignorant and unreasoning prejudice, they lack the true spirit of the slavery-destroying revolutionary movement.

The voice of Socialism must be as inspiring music to the ears of those in bondage, especially the weak black brethren, doubly enslaved, who are bowed to the earth and groan in despair beneath the burden of the centuries.

For myself, my heart goes to the Negro and I make no apology to any white man for it. In fact, when I see the poor, brutalized, outraged black victim, I feel a burning sense of guilt for his intellectual poverty and moral debasement that makes me blush for the unspeakable crimes committed by my own race.

In closing, permit me to express the hope that the next convention may repeal the resolutions on the Negro question. The Negro does not need them and they serve to increase rather than diminish the necessity for explanation.

We have nothing special to offer the Negro, and we cannot make separate appeals to all the races.

The Socialist party is the party of the working class, regardless of color—the whole working class of the whole world.

WOMAN-COMRADE AND EQUAL[2]

The *London Saturday Review* in a recent issue brutally said: "Man's superiority is shown by his ability to keep woman in subjection." Such a sentiment is enough to kindle the wrath of every man who loves his wife or reveres his mother. It is the voice of the wilderness, the snarl of the primitive. Measured by that standard, every tyrant has been a hero, and brutality is at once the acme of perfection and the glory of man.

[2] Pamphlet published by the Socialist Party, Chicago, Ill., undated.

Real men do not utter such sentiments. He who does so prostitutes his powers and links himself once more to the chattering ape that wrenches the neck of the cowering female, glorying as he does so in the brute force that is his.

Yet the sentiment is not confined to a moral degenerate, who writes lies for pay, or to sycophants who sell their souls for the crumbs that arrogant wealth doles out to its vassals. It is embodied and embedded in the cruel system under which we live, the criminal system which grinds children to profits in the mills, which in the sweatshops saps women of their power to mother a race of decent men, which traps the innocent and true-hearted, making them worse than slaves in worse than all that has been said of hell. It finds expression in premiers hiding from petticoated agitators, in presidents ignoring the pleading of the mothers of men, in the clubbing and jailing of suffragettes; in Wall Street gamblers and brigands cackling from their piles of loot at the demands of justice. It is expressed in laws which rank mothers and daughters as idiots and criminals. It writes, beside the declaration that men should rebel against taxation without representation, that women must submit to taxation without representation. It makes property the god that men worship, and says that woman shall have no property rights. Instead of that, she herself is counted as property, living by sufferance of the man who doles out the pittance that she uses.

Woman is made the slave of a slave, and is reckoned fit only for companionship in lust. The hands and breasts that nursed all men to life are scorned as the forgetful brute proclaims his superior strength and plumes himself that he can subjugate the one who made him what he is, and would have made him better had customs and institutions permitted.

How differently is woman regarded by the truly wise and the really great! Paolo Lombroso, one of the deepest students of mind that time has ripened, says of her:

> The most simple, most frivolous and thoughtless woman hides at the bottom of her soul a spark of heroism, which neither she herself nor anybody else suspects, which she never shows if her life runs its normal course, but which springs into evidence and manifests itself by actions of devotion and self-sacrifice, if fate strikes her or those whom she loves. Then she does not wince, she does not complain nor give way to useless despair, but rushes into the breach. The woman who hesitates to put her feet into cold, placid water throws herself into the perils of the roaring, surging maelstrom.

Sardou, the analytical novelist, declares:

> I consider women superior to men in almost everything. They possess intuitive faculty to an extraordinary degree, and may almost always

be trusted to do the right thing in the right place. They are full of noble instincts, and, though heavily handicapped by fate, come well out of every ordeal. You have only to turn to history to learn the truth of what I say.

Lester F. Ward, the economist, the subtle student of affairs, gives this testimony:

> We have no conception of the real amount of talent or of genius possessed by women. It is probably not greatly inferior to that of man even now, and a few generations of enlightened opinion on the subject, if shared by both sexes, would perhaps show that the difference is qualitative only.

I am glad to align myself with a party that declares for absolute equality between the sexes. Anything less than this is too narrow for twentieth-century civilization, and too small for a man who has a right conception of manhood.

Let us grant that woman has not reached the full height which she might attain—when I think of her devotion to duty, her tender ministries, her gentle spirit that in the clash and struggle of passion has made her the savior of the world, the thought, so far from making me decry womanhood, gives me the vision of a race so superior as to cause me to wonder at its glory and beauty ineffable.

Man has not reached his best. He never will reach his best until he walks the upward way side by side with woman. Plato was right in his fancy that man and woman are merely halves of humanity, each requiring the qualities of the other in order to attain the highest character. Shakespeare understood it when he made his noblest women strong as men and his best men tender as women.

Under our brutal forms of existence, beating womanhood to dust, we have raged in passion for the individual woman, for use only. Some day we shall develop the social passion for womanhood, and then the gross will disappear in service and justice and companionship. Then we shall lift woman from the mire where our fists have struck her, and set her by our side as our comrade and equal and that will be love indeed.

Man's superiority will be shown, not in the fact that he has enslaved his wife, but in that he has made her free.

7

Antiwar Leader and Victim
of Government Repression

During World War I, Debs became a symbol of the Socialist party's uncompromising opposition to the war. The speech he delivered in Canton, Ohio, was typical of the presentations Debs and other Socialists were making. This particular speech, however, led to government indictment for violation of the Espionage Act. Deb's address to the jury and his statement to the court during his trial reveal that Debs used the courtroom to wage a political fight. His appeal was to those outside the jury room, since he understood that according to the terms of the law, he was indeed guilty. Debs felt that it was not himself and the Socialists who were on trial in Ohio, but the most basic American institutions.

THE CANTON, OHIO SPEECH [1]

Comrades, friends, and fellow workers, for this very cordial greeting, this very hearty reception, I thank you all with the fullest appreciation of your interest in and your devotion to the cause for which I am to speak to you this afternoon.

To speak for labor, to plead the cause of the men and women and children who toil, to serve the working class has always been to me a high privilege, a duty of love.

I have just returned from a visit over yonder (pointing to the workhouse), where three of our most loyal comrades* are paying the penalty for their devotion to the cause of the working class. They have come to realize, as many of us have, that it is extremely dangerous to exercise the constitutional right of free speech in a country fighting to make democracy safe in the world.

I realize that, in speaking to you this afternoon, there are certain

---

[1] Delivered at Nimisilla Park, Canton, Ohio, Sunday afternoon, June 16th, 1918. This speech as printed is an abridgement of the original. Omissions consist solely of local and out-of-date references and repetitions.

* Debs refers to three Cleveland Socialists, Charles E. Ruthenberg, Alfred Wagenknecht, and Charles Baker, imprisoned because of their opposition to the war.

limitations placed upon the right of free speech. I must be exceedingly careful, prudent, as to what I say, and even more careful and prudent as to how I say it. I may not be able to say all I think, but I am not going to say anything that I do not think. I would rather a thousand times be a free soul in jail than to be a sycophant and coward in the streets. They may put those boys in jail—and some of the rest of us in jail—but they cannot put the Socialist movement in jail. Those prison bars separate their bodies from ours, but their souls are here this afternoon. They are simply paying the penalty that all men have paid in all the ages of history for standing erect, and for seeking to pave the way to better conditions for mankind.

If it had not been for the men and women, who, in the past, have had the moral courage to go to jail, we would still be in the jungles. . . .

There is but one thing you have to be concerned about, and that is that you keep four-square with the principles of the international Socialist movement. It is only when you begin to compromise that trouble begins. So far as I am concerned, it does not matter what others may say, or think, or do, as long as I am sure that I am right with myself and the cause. There are so many who seek refuge in the popular side of a great question. As a Socialist, I have long since learned how to stand alone. . . .

I never had much faith in leaders. I am willing to be charged with almost anything, rather than to be charged with being a leader. I am suspicious of leaders, and especially of the intellectual variety. Give me the rank and file every day in the week. If you go to the city of Washington, and you examine the pages of the Congressional Directory, you will find that almost all of those corporation lawyers and cowardly politicians, members of Congress, and misrepresentatives of the masses—you will find that almost all of them claim, in glowing terms, that they have risen from the ranks to places of eminence and distinction. I am very glad I cannot make that claim for myself. I would be ashamed to admit that I had risen from the ranks. When I rise it will be with the ranks, and not from the ranks. . . .

They who have been reading the capitalist newspapers realize what a capacity they have for lying. We have been reading them lately. They know all about the Socialist party . . . except what is true. Only the other day they took an article that I had written—and most of you have read it—most of you members of the party, at least—and they made it appear that I had undergone a marvelous transformation. I had suddenly become changed—had in fact come to my senses; I had ceased to be a wicked Socialist, and had become a respectable Socialist, a patriotic Socialist—as if I had ever been anything else.

What was the purpose of this deliberate misrepresentation? It is so self-evident that it suggests itself. The purpose was to sow the seeds of dissension in our ranks; to have it appear that we were divided among ourselves; that we were pitted against each other, to our mutual undoing. But Socialists were not born yesterday. They know how to read capitalist newspapers, and to believe exactly the opposite of what they read.

Why should a Socialist be discouraged on the eve of the greatest triumph in all the history of the Socialist movement? It is true that these are anxious, trying days for us all—testing days for the women and men who are upholding the banner of labor in the struggle of the working class of all the world against the exploiters of all the world; a time in which the weak and cowardly will falter and fail and desert. They lack the fiber to endure the revolutionary test; they fall away; they disappear as if they had never been. On the other hand, they who are animated by the unconquerable spirit of the social revolution; they who have the moral courage to stand erect and assert their convictions; stand by them; fight for them; go to jail or to hell for them, if need be— they are writing their names, in this crucial hour—they are writing their names in fadeless letters in the history of mankind. . . .

Are we opposed to Prussian militarism? Why, we have been fighting it since the day the Socialist movement was born; and we are going to continue to fight it, day and night, until it is wiped from the face of the earth. Between us there is no truce—no compromise.

But, before I proceed along this line, let me recall a little history, in which I think we are all interested.

In 1869 that grand old warrior of the social revolution, the elder Liebknecht, was arrested and sentenced to prison for three months, because of his war, as a Socialist, on the Kaiser and on the Junkers that rule Germany. In the meantime the Franco-Prussian war broke out. Liebknecht and Bebel were the Socialist members in the Reichstag. They were the only two who had the courage to protest against taking Alsace-Lorraine from France and annexing it to Germany. And for this they were sentenced two years to a prison fortress charged with high treason; because, even in that early day, almost fifty years ago, these leaders, these forerunners of the international Socialist movement were fighting the Kaiser and fighting the Junkers of Germany. They have continued to fight them from that day to this. Multiplied thousands of Socialists have languished in the jails of Germany because of their heroic warface upon the despotic ruling class of that country. . . .

I hate, I loathe, I despise Junkers and junkerdom. I have no earthly use for the Junkers of Germany, and not one particle more use for the Junkers in the United States.

They tell us that we live in a great free republic; that our institutions are democratic; that we are a free and self-governing people. This is too much, even for a joke. But it is not a subject for levity; it is an exceedingly serious matter.

To whom do the Wall Street Junkers in our country marry their daughters? After they have wrung their countless millions from your sweat, your agony and your life's blood, in a time of war as in a time of peace, they invest these untold millions in the purchase of titles of broken-down aristocrats, such as princes, dukes, counts, and other parasites and no-accounts. Would they be satisfied to wed their daughters to honest workingmen? To real democrats? Oh, no! They scour the markets of Europe for vampires who are titled and nothing else. And they swap their millions for the titles, so that matrimony with them becomes literally a matter of money.

These are the gentry who are today wrapped up in the American flag, who shout their claim from the housetops that they are the only patriots, and who have their magnifying glasses in hand, scanning the country for evidence of disloyalty, eager to apply the brand of treason to the men who dare to even whisper their opposition to junker rule in the United States. No wonder Sam Johnson declared that "patriotism is the last refuge of the scoundrel." He must have had this Wall Street gentry in mind, or at least their prototypes, for in every age it has been the tyrant, the oppressor, and the exploiter who has wrapped himself in the cloak of patriotism, or religion, or both to deceive and overawe the people. . . .

I know Tom Mooney intimately—as if he were my own brother. He is an absolutely honest man. He had no more to do with the crime with which he was charged and for which he was convicted than I had. And if he ought to go to the gallows, so ought I. If he is guilty every man who belongs to a labor organization or to the Socialist party is likewise guilty.

What is Tom Mooney guilty of? I will tell you. I am familiar with his record. For years he has been fighting bravely and without compromise the battles of the working class out on the Pacific coast. He refused to be bribed and he could not be browbeaten. In spite of all attempts to intimidate him he continued loyally in the service of the organized workers, and for this he became a marked man. The henchmen of the powerful and corrupt corporations concluding finally that he could not be bought or bribed or bullied, decided he must therefore be murdered. That is why Tom Mooney is today a life prisoner, and why he would have been hanged as a felon long years ago but for the world-wide protest of the working class. . . .

Who appoints our federal judges? The people? In all the history of the country, the working class have never named a federal judge. There are 121 of these judges and every solitary one holds his position, his tenure, through the influence and power of corporate capital. The corporations and trusts dictate their appointment. And when they go to the bench, they go, not to serve the people, but to serve the interests that place them and keep them where they are.

Why, the other day, by a vote of five to four—a kind of craps game—come seven, come 'leven—they declared the child labor law unconstitutional—a law secured after twenty years of education and agitation on the part of all kinds of people. And yet, by a majority of one, the Supreme Court, a body of corporation lawyers, with just one exception, wiped that law from the statute books, and this in our so-called Democracy, so that we may continue to grind the flesh and blood and bones of puny little children into profits for the junkers of Wall Street. And this in a country that boasts of fighting to make the world safe for democracy! The history of this country is being written in the blood of the childhood the industrial lords have murdered. . . .

How stupid and short-sighted the ruling class really is! Cupidity is stone blind. It has no vision. The greedy, profit-seeking exploiter cannot see beyond the end of his nose. He can see a chance for an "opening"; he is cunning enough to know what graft is and where it is, and how it can be secured, but vision he has none—not the slightest. He knows nothing of the great throbbing world that spreads out in all directions. He has no capacity for literature; no appreciation of art; no soul for beauty. That is the penalty the parasites pay for the violation of the laws of life. . . . Every move they make in their game of greed but hastens their own doom. Every blow they strike at the Socialist movement reacts upon themselves. Every time they strike at us, they hit themselves. It never fails. Every time they strangle a Socialist paper they add a thousand voices proclaiming the truth of the principles of Socialism and the ideals of the Socialist movement. They help us in spite of themselves.

Socialism is a growing idea, an expanding philosophy. It is spreading over the entire face of the earth. It is as vain to resist it as it would be to arrest the sunrise on the morrow. It is coming, coming, coming all along the line. Can you not see it? If not, I advise you to consult an oculist. There is certainly something the matter with your vision. It is the mightiest movement in the history of mankind. What a privilege to serve it! I have regretted a thousand times that I can do so little for the movement that has done so much for me. The little that I am, the little that I am hoping to be, I owe to the Socialist movement. It has given me my ideas and ideals, my principles and convictions, and I would not exchange one of them for all of Rockefeller's blood-stained dollars. It has taught me how to serve—a lesson to me of priceless value. It has taught me the ecstasy in the handclasp of a comrade. It has enabled me to hold high communion with you, and made it possible for me to take my place side by side with you in the great struggle for the better day; to multiply myself over and over again; to thrill with a fresh-born manhood; to feel life truly worth while; to open new avenues of vision; to spread out glorious vistas; to know that I am kin to all that throbs; to be class-conscious, and to realize that, regardless of nationality, race, creed, color, or sex, every man, every woman who toils, who renders useful service, every member of the working class without an exception, is my comrade, my brother and sister—and that to serve them and their cause is the highest duty of my life. . . .

Yes, my comrades, my heart is attuned to yours. Aye, all our hearts now throb as one great heart responsive to the battle cry of the social revolution. Here, in this alert and inspiring assemblage our hearts are with the Bolsheviki of Russia. Those heroic men and women, those unconquerable comrades have by their incomparable valor and sacrifice added fresh lustre to the fame of the international movement. . . . The very first act of the triumphant Russian revolution was to proclaim a state of peace with all mankind, coupled with a fervent moral appeal, not to kings, not to emperors, rulers or diplomats, but to *the people* of all nations. . . . When the Bolsheviki came into power and went through the archives they found and exposed the secret treaties— the treaties that were made between the Czar and the French Government, the British Government and the Italian Government, proposing, after the victory was achieved, to dismember the German Empire and destroy the Central Powers. These treaties have never been denied nor repudiated. Very little has been said about them in the American press. I have a copy of these treaties, showing that the purpose of the Allies is exactly the purpose of the Central Powers, and that is the conquest and spoliation of the weaker nations that has always been the purpose of war.

Wars throughout history have been waged for conquest and plunder. In the Middle Ages when the feudal lords who inhabited the castles whose towers may still be seen along the Rhine concluded to enlarge their domains, to increase their power, their prestige, and their wealth they declared war upon one another. But they themselves did not go to war any more than the modern feudal lords, the barons of Wall Street go to war. The feudal barons of the Middle Ages, the economic predecessors of the capitalists of our day, declared all wars. And their miserable serfs fought all the battles. The poor, ignorant serfs had been taught to revere their masters; to believe that when their masters declared war upon one another, it was their patriotic duty to fall upon one another and to cut one another's throats for the profit and glory of the lords and barons who held them in contempt. And that is war in a nutshell. The master class has always declared the wars; the subject class has always fought the battles. The master class has had all to gain and nothing to lose, while the subject class has had nothing to gain and all to lose—especially their lives. . . .

And here let me emphasize the fact—and it cannot be repeated, too often—that the working class who fight all the battles, the working class who make the supreme sacrifices, the working class who freely shed their blood and furnish the corpses, have never yet had a voice in either declaring war or making peace. It is the ruling class that invariably does both. They alone declare war and they alone make peace.

> Yours not to reason why;
> Yours but to do and die.

That is their motto and we object on the part of the awakening workers of this nation. . . .

What a compliment it is to the Socialist movement to be persecuted for the sake of the truth! The truth alone will make the people free. And for this reason the truth must not be permitted to reach the people. The truth has always been dangerous to the rule of the rogue, the exploiter, the robber. So the truth must be ruthlessly suppressed. That is why they are trying to detroy the Socialist movement; and every time they strike a blow they add a thousand new voices to the hosts proclaiming that Socialism is the hope of humanity and has come to emancipate the people from their final form of servitude. . . .

We do not attack individuals. We do not seek to avenge ourselves upon those opposed to our faith. We have no fight with individuals as such. We are capable of pitying those who hate us. We do not hate them; we know better; we would freely give them a cup of water if they needed it. There is no room in our hearts for hate, except for the system, the social system in which it is possible for one man to amass a stupendous fortune doing nothing, while millions of others suffer and struggle and agonize and die for the bare necessities of existence. . . .

It is the minorities who have made the history of this world. It is the few who have had the courage to take their places at the front, who have been true enough to themselves to speak the truth that was in them, who have dared oppose the established order of things, who have espoused the cause of the suffering, struggling poor, who have upheld without regard to personal consequences the cause of freedom and righteousness. It is they, the heroic, self-sacrificing few who have made the history of the race and who have paved the way from barbarism to civilization. The many prefer to remain upon the popular side. They lack the courage and vision to join a despised minority that stands for a principle; they have not the moral fiber that withstands, endures, and finally conquers. They are to be pitied and not treated with contempt for they cannot help their cowardice. But, thank God, in every age and in every nation there have been the brave and self-reliant few, and they have been sufficient to their historic task; and we, who are here today, are under infinite obligations to them because they suffered, they sacrificed, they went to jail, they had their bones broken upon the wheel, they were burned at the stake and their ashes scattered to the winds by the hands of hate and revenge in their struggle to leave the world better for us than they found it for themselves. We are under eternal obligations to them because of what they did and what they suffered for us and the only way we can discharge that obligation is by doing the best we can for those who are to come after us. . . .

The heart of the International Socialist never beats a retreat.

They are pressing forward, here, there and everywhere, in all the zones that girdle the globe. Everywhere these awakening workers, these class-conscious proletarians, these hardy sons and daughters of honest toil are proclaiming the glad tidings of the coming emancipation; everywhere their hearts are attuned to the most sacred cause that ever challenged men and women to action in all the history of the world. Everywhere they are moving toward democracy and the dawn; marching toward the sunrise, their faces all aglow with the light of the coming day. These are the Socialists, the most zealous and enthusiastic crusaders the world has ever known. They are making history that will light up the horizon of coming generations, for their mission is the emancipation of the human race. They have been reviled; they have been ridiculed, persecuted, imprisoned, and have suffered death, but they have been sufficient to themselves and their cause, and their final triumph is but a question of time. . . .

If you would be respected you have got to begin by respecting yourself. Stand up squarely and look yourself in the face and see a man! Do not allow yourself to fall into the predicament of the poor fellow who, after he had heard a Socialist speech concluded that he too ought to be a Socialist. The argument he had heard was unanswerable. "Yes," he said to himself, "all the speaker said was true and I certainly ought to join the party." But after a while he allowed his ardor to cool and he soberly concluded that by joining the party he might anger his boss and lose his job. He then concluded: "I can't take the chance." That night he slept alone. There was something on his conscience and it resulted in a dreadful dream. Men always have such dreams when they betray themselves. A Socialist is free to go to bed with a clear conscience. He goes to sleep with his manhood and he awakens and walks forth in the morning with his self-respect. He is unafraid and he can look the whole world in the face without a tremor and without a blush. But this poor weakling who lacked the courage to do the bidding of his reason and conscience was haunted by a startling dream and at midnight he awoke in terror, bounded from his bed and exclaimed: "My God, there is nobody in this room." He was absolutely right. There was nobody in that room.

How would you like to sleep in a room that had nobody in it? It is an awful thing to be nobody. That is certainly a state of mind to get out of, the sooner the better. . . .

To turn your back on the corrupt Republican party and the corrupt Democratic party—the gold-dust lackeys of the ruling class counts for something. It counts for still more after you have stepped out of those popular and corrupt capitalist parties to join a minority party that has an ideal, that stands for a principle, and fights for a cause. This will be the most important change you have ever made and the time will come when you will thank me for having made the suggestion. It was the day of days for me. I remember it well. It was like passing from midnight darkness to the noontide light of day. It came almost like a flash and found me ready. It must have been in such a flash that great, seething, throbbing Russia, prepared by centuries of slavery and tears and martyrdom, was transformed from a dark continent to a land of living light.

There is something splendid, something sustaining and inspiring in the prompting of the heart to be true to yourself and to the best you know, especially in a crucial hour of your life. You are in the crucible today, my Socialist comrades! You are going to be tried by fire, to what extent no one knows. If you are weak-fibered and faint-hearted you will be lost to the Socialist movement. We will have to bid you good-bye. You are not the stuff of which revolutions are made. We are sorry for you unless you chance to be an "intellectual." The "intellectuals," many of them, are already gone. No loss on our side nor gain on the other.

I am always amused in the discussion of the "intellectual" phase of this question. It is the same old standard under which the rank and file are judged. What would become of the sheep if they had no shepherd to lead them out of the wilderness into the land of milk and honey?

Oh, yes, "I am your shepherd and ye are my mutton."

They would have us believe that if we had no "intellectuals" we would have no movement. They would have our party, the rank and file, controlled by the "intellectual" bosses as the Republican and Democratic parties are controlled. These capitalist parties are managed by "intellectual" leaders and the rank and file are sheep that follow the bellwether to the shambles. . . .

The capitalist system affects to have great regard and reward for intellect, and the capitalists give themselves full credit for having superior brains. When we have ventured to say that the time would come when the working class would rule they have bluntly answered "Never! it requires brains to rule." The workers of course have none. And they certainly try hard to prove it by proudly supporting the political parties of their masters under whose administration they are kept in poverty and servitude. . . .

It is true that they have the brains that indicates the cunning of the fox, the wolf, but as for brains denoting real intelligence and the measure of intellectual capacity they are the most woefully ignorant people on earth. Give me a hundred capitalists and let me ask them a dozen simple questions about the history of their own country and I will prove to you that they are as ignorant and unlettered as any you may find in the so-called lower class. They know little of history; they are strangers to science; they are ignorant of sociology and blind to art but they know how to exploit, how to gouge, how to rob, and do it with legal sanction. They always proceed legally for the reason that the class which has the power to rob upon a large scale has also the power to control the government and legalize their robbery. I regret that lack of time prevents me from discussing this phase of the question more at length.

They are continually talking about your patriotic duty. It is not *their* but *your* patriotic duty that they are concerned about. There is a decided difference. Their patriotic duty never takes them to the firing line or chucks them into the trenches.

And now among other things they are urging you to "cultivate" war gardens, while at the same time a government war report just issued shows that practically 52 percent of the arable, tillable soil is held out of use by the landlords, speculators, and profiteers. They themselves do not cultivate the soil. They could not if they would. Nor do they allow others to cultivate it. They keep it idle to enrich themselves, to pocket the millions of dollars of unearned increment. Who is it that makes this land valuable while it is fenced in and kept out of use? It is the people. Who pockets this tremendous accumulation of value? The landlords. And these landlords who toil not and spin not are supreme among American "patriots."

In passing I suggest that we stop a moment to think about the term "landlords." "LANDLORD!" Lord of the Land! The Lord of the land is indeed a super-patriot. This lord who practically owns the earth tells you that we are fighting this war to make the world safe for democracy —he, who shuts out all humanity from his private domain; he, who profiteers at the expense of the people who have been slain and mutilated by multiplied thousands, under pretense of being the great Americans patriot. It is he, this identical patriot who is in fact the archenemy of the people; it is he that you need to wipe from power. It is he who is a far greater menace to your liberty and your well-being than the Prussian junkers on the other side of the Atlantic Ocean.

Fifty-two percent of the land kept out of use, according to their own figures! They tell you that there is an alarming shortage of flour and that you need to produce more. They tell you further that you have got to save wheat so that more can be exported for the soldiers who are fighting on the other side, while half of your tillable soil is held out of use by the landlords and profiteers. What do you think of that? . . .

Let us illustrate a vital point. Here is the coal in great deposits all about us; here are the miners and the machinery of production. Why should there be a coal famine upon the one hand and an army of idle and hungry miners on the other hand? Is it not an incredibly stupid situation, an almost idiotic if not criminal state of affairs?

In the present system the miner, a wage-slave, gets down into a pit three or four hundred feet deep. He works hard and produces a ton of coal. But he does not own an ounce of it. That coal belongs to some mine-owning plutocrat who may be in New York or sailing the high seas in his private yacht; or he may be hobnobbing with royalty in the capitals of Europe, and that is where most of them were before the war was declared. The industrial captain, so-called, who lives in Paris, London, Vienna, or some other center of gayety, does not have to work to revel in luxury. He owns the mines and he might as well own the miners.

That is where you workers are and where you will remain as long as you give your support to the political parties of your masters and exploiters. You vote these miners out of a job and reduce them to corporation vassals and paupers.

We Socialists say: "Take possession of the mines in the name of the people." Set the miners at work and give every miner the equivalent of all the coal he produces. Reduce the work day in proportion to the development of productive machinery. That would at once settle the matter of a coal famine and of idle miners. But that is too simple a proposition and the people will have none of it. The time will come, however, when the people will be driven to take such action for there is no other efficient and permanent solution of the problem. . . .

Of course that would be Socialism as far as it goes. But you are not in favor of that program. It is too visionary because it is so simple and practical. So you will have to continue to wait until winter is upon you before you get your coal and then pay three prices for it because you insist upon voting a capitalist ticket and giving your support to the present wage-slave system. The trouble with you is that you are still in a capitalist state of mind.

Lincoln said: "If you want that thing, that is the thing you want";

and you will get it to your heart's content. But some good day you will wake up and realize that a change is needed and wonder why you did not know it long before. Yes, a change is certainly needed, not merely a change of party but a change of system; a change from slavery to freedom and from despotism to democracy, wide as the world. When this change comes at last, we shall rise from brutehood to brotherhood, and to accomplish it we have to educate and organize the workers industrially and politically. . . .

There are few men who have the courage to say a word in favor of the IWW. I have. Let me say here that I have great respect for the IWW. Far greater than I have for their infamous detractors.

It is only necessary to label a man "IWW" to have him lynched. War makes possible all such crimes and outrages. And war comes in spite of the people. When Wall Street says war the press says war and the pulpit promptly follows with its *Amen.* In every age the pulpit has been on the side of the rulers and not on the side of the people. That is one reason why the preachers so fiercely denounce the IWW. . . .

Political action and industrial action must supplement and sustain each other. You will never vote the Socialist republic into existence. You will have to lay its foundations in industrial organization. The industrial union is the forerunner of industrial democracy. In the shop where the workers are associated is where industrial democracy has its beginning. Organize according to your industries! Get together in every department of industrial service! United and acting together for the common good your power is invincible.

When you have organized industrially you will soon learn that you can manage as well as operate industry. You will soon realize that you do not need the idle masters and exploiters. They are simply parasites. They do not employ you as you imagine but you employ them to take from you what you produce, and that is how they function in industry. You can certainly dispense with them in that capacity. You do not need them to depend upon for your jobs. You can never be free while you work and live by their sufferance. You must own your own tools and then you will control your own jobs, enjoy the products of your own labor and be free men instead of industrial slaves.

Organize industrially and make your organization complete. Then unite in the Socialist party. Vote as you strike and strike as you vote.

Your union and your party embrace the working class. The Socialist party expresses the interest, hopes, and aspirations of the toilers of all the world.

Get your fellow workers into the industrial union and the political party to which they rightfully belong, especially this year, this historic year in which the forces of labor will assert themselves as they never have before. This is the year that calls for men and women who have the courage, the manhood, and womanhood to do their duty.

Get into the Socialist party and take your place in its ranks; help to inspire the weak and strengthen the faltering, and do your share to speed the coming of the brighter and better day for us all.

When we unite and act together on the industrial field and when we vote together on election day we shall develop the supreme power of the one class that can and will bring permanent peace to the world. We shall then have the intelligence, the courage, and the power for our great task. In due time industry will be organized on a cooperative basis. We shall conquer the public power. We shall then transfer the title deeds of the railroads, the telegraph lines, the mines, mills, and great industries to the people in their collective capacity; we shall take possession of all these social utilities in the name of the people. We shall then have industrial democracy. We shall be a free nation whose government is of and by and for the people.

And now for all of us to do our duty! The clarion call is ringing in our ears and we cannot falter without being convicted of treason to ourselves and to our great cause.

Do not worry over the charge of treason to your masters, but be concerned about the treason that involves yourselves. Be true to yourself and you cannot be a traitor to any good cause on earth.

Yes, in good time we are going to sweep into power in this nation and throughout the world. We are going to destroy all enslaving and degrading capitalist institutions and recreate them as free and humanizing institutions. The world is daily changing before our eyes. The sun of capitalism is setting; the sun of Socialism is rising. It is our duty to build the new nation and the free republic. We need industrial and social builders. We Socialists are the builders of the beautiful world that is to be. We are all pledged to do our part. We are inviting—aye challenging you in the name of your own manhood and womanhood to join us and do your part.

In due time the hour will strike and this great cause triumphant —the greatest in history—will proclaim the emancipation of the working class and the brotherhood of all mankind.

ADDRESS TO THE JURY [2]

Gentlemen, I do not fear you in this hour of accusation, nor do I shrink from the consequences of my utterances or my acts. Standing

[2] On September 12th, 1918, Debs was convicted of having violated the Espionage Law in a speech delivered at Canton. On September 14th, he was sentenced to ten years in prison. At the close of the Government's case, in the trial, Debs refused

before you, charged as I am with crime, I can yet look the court in the face, I can look you in the face, I can look the world in the face, for in my conscience, in my soul, there is festering no accusation of guilt. . . .

I wish to admit the truth of all that has been testified to in this proceeding. I have no disposition to deny anything that is true. I would not, if I could, escape the results of an adverse verdict. I would not retract a word that I have uttered that I believe to be true to save myself from going to the penitentiary for the rest of my days.

Gentlemen, you have heard the report of my speech at Canton on June 16th, and I submit that there is not a word in that speech to warrant the charges set out in the indictment. I admit having delivered the speech. I admit the accuracy of the speech in all of its main features as reported in this proceeding.

In what I had to say there my purpose was to have the people understand something about the social system in which we live and to prepare them to change this system by perfectly peaceable and orderly means into what I, as a Socialist, conceive to be a real democracy.

From what you heard in the address of the counsel for the prosecution, you might naturally infer that I am an advocate of force and violence. It is not true. I have never advocated violence in any form. I have always believed in education, in intelligence, in enlightenment, and I have always made my appeal to the reason and to the conscience of the people.

I admit being opposed to the present social system. I am doing what little I can, and have been for many years, to bring about a change that shall do away with the rule of the great body of the people by a relatively small class and establish in this country an industrial and social democracy.

When great changes occur in history, when great principles are involved, as a rule the majority are wrong. The minority are usually right. In every age there have been a few heroic souls who have been in advance of their time, who have been misunderstood, maligned, persecuted, sometimes put to death. Long after their martyrdom monuments were erected to them and garlands woven from their graves. . . .

A century and a half ago when the American colonists were still

---

to allow any witnesses to be put on in his defense and through his chief counsel, Stedman, announced that he would plead his own cause to the jury. The case was appealed to the Supreme Court of the United States to test the constitutionaliy of those sections of the Espionage Law under which the indictment was returned. Debs was given his liberty on bond of ten thousand dollars pending final action by the higher court. The speech to the jury and the address to the court herein printed are somewhat abridged.

foreign subjects; when there were a few men who had faith in the common people and their destiny, and believed that they could rule themselves without a king; in that day to question the divine right of the king to rule was treason. If you will read Bancroft or any other American historian, you will find that a great majority of the colonists were loyal to the king and actually believed that he had a divine right to rule over them. . . . But there were a few men in that day who said, "We don't need a king; we can govern ourselves." And they began an agitation that has immortalized them in history.

Washington, Jefferson, Franklin, Paine, and their compeers were the rebels of their day. When they began to chafe under the rule of a foreign king and to sow the seed of resistance among the colonists they were opposed by the people and denounced by the press. . . . But they had the moral courage to be true to their convictions, to stand erect and defy all the forces of reaction and detraction; and that is why their names shine in history, and why the great respectable majority of their day sleep in forgotten graves. . . .

It was my good fortune to personally know Wendell Phillips. I heard the story of his cruel and cowardly persecution from his own eloquent lips just a little while before they were silenced in death.

William Lloyd Garrison, Wendell Phillips, Elizabeth Cady Stanton, Susan B. Anthony, Gerrit Smith, Thaddeus Stevens, and other leaders of the abolition movement who were regarded as public enemies and treated accordingly, were true to their faith and stood their ground. They are all in history. You are now teaching your children to revere their memories, while all of their detractors are in oblivion.

Chattel slavery has disappeared. But we are not yet free. We are engaged today in another mighty agitation. It is as wide as the world. It means the rise of the toiling masses who are gradually becoming conscious of their interests, their power, and their mission as a class; who are organizing industrially and politically and who are slowly but surely developing the economic and political power that is to set them free. . . .

From the beginning of the war to this day I have never by word or act been guilty of the charges embraced in this indictment. If I have criticized, if I have condemned, it is because I believed it to be my duty, and that it was my right to do so under the laws of the land. I have had ample precedents for my attitude. This country has been engaged in a number of wars and every one of them has been condemned by some of the people, among them some of the most eminent men of their time. . . .

The revolutionary fathers who had been oppressed under king's rule understood that free speech, a free press, and the right of free assemblage by the people were fundamental principles in democratic government. The very first amendment to the Constitution reads:

> Congress shall make no law respecting an establishment of religion, or prohibiting the free exercise thereof; or abridging the freedom of speech, or of the press; or the right of the people peaceably to assemble, and to petition the government for a redress of grievances.

That is perfectly plain English. It can be understood by a child. I believe the revolutionary fathers meant just what is here stated— that Congress shall make no law abridging the freedom of speech or of the press, or of the right of the people to peaceably assemble, and to petition the government for a redress of their grievances.

That is the right I exercised at Canton on the 16th day of last June; and for the exercise of that right, I now have to answer to this indictment. I believe in the right of free speech, in war as well as in peace. I would not under any circumstances gag the lips of my bitterest enemy. I would under no circumstances suppress free speech. It is far more dangerous to attempt to gag the people than to allow them to speak freely what is in their hearts.

I have told you that I am no lawyer, but it seems to me that I know enough to know that if Congress enacts any law that conflicts with this provision in the Constitution, that law is void. If the Espionage Law finally stands, then the Constitution of the United States is dead. . . .

I cannot take back a word I have said. I cannot repudiate a sentence I have uttered. I stand before you guilty of having made this speech. I do not know, I cannot tell, what your verdict may be; nor does it matter much, so far as I am concerned.

I am the smallest part of this trial. I have lived long enough to realize my own personal insignificance in relation to a great issue that involves the welfare of the whole people. What you may choose to do to me will be of small consequence after all. I am not on trial here. There is an infinitely greater issue that is being tried today in this court, though you may not be conscious of it. American institutions are on trial here before a court of American citizens. The future will render the final verdict.

And now, your honor, permit me to return my thanks for your patient consideration. And to you, gentlemen of the jury, for the kindness with which you have listened to me.

I am prepared for your verdict.

STATEMENT TO THE COURT [3]

Your Honor, years ago I recognized my kinship with all living beings, and I made up my mind that I was not one bit better than the meanest on earth. I said then, and I say now, that while there is a lower class, I am in it, while there is a criminal element I am of it, and while there is a soul in prison, I am not free.

I listened to all that was said in this court in support and justification of this prosecution, but my mind remains unchanged. I look upon the Espionage Law as a despotic enactment in flagrant conflict with democratic principles and with the spirit of free institutions. . . .

Your Honor, I have stated in this court that I am opposed to the social system in which we live; that I believe in a fundamental change —but if possible by peaceable and orderly means. . . .

Standing here this morning, I recall my boyhood. At fourteen I went to work in a railroad shop; at sixteen I was firing a freight engine on a railroad. I remember all the hardships and privations of that earlier day, and from that time until now my heart has been with the working class. I could have been in Congress long ago. I have preferred to go to prison. . . .

I am thinking this morning of the men in the mills and factories; of the men in the mines and on the railroads. I am thinking of the women who for a paltry wage are compelled to work out their barren lives; of the little children who in this system are robbed of their childhood and in their tender years are seized in the remorseless grasp of Mammon and forced into the industrial dungeons, there to feed the monster machines while they themselves are being starved and stunted, body and soul. I see them dwarfed and diseased and their little lives broken and blasted because in this high noon of our twentieth-century Christian civilization money is still so much more important than the flesh and blood of childhood. In very truth gold is god today and rules with pitiless sway in the affairs of men.

In this country—the most favored beneath the bending skies—we have vast areas of the richest and most fertile soil, material resources in inexhaustible abundance, the most marvelous productive machinery on earth, and millions of eager workers ready to apply their labor to that machinery to produce in abundance for every man, woman, and child—and if there are still vast numbers of our people who are the victims of poverty and whose lives are an unceasing struggle all the

[3] After a motion for a new trial had been overruled, Debs was asked if he had anything to say before sentence was passed on him.

way from youth to old age, until at last death comes to their rescue and stills their aching hearts and lulls these hapless victims to dreamless sleep, it is not the fault of the Almighty: it cannot be charged to nature, but it is due entirely to the outgrown social system in which we live that ought to be abolished not only in the interest of the toiling masses but in the higher interest of all humanity. . . .

I believe, Your Honor, in common with all Socialists, that this nation ought to own and control its own industries. I believe, as all Socialists do, that all things that are jointly needed and used ought to be jointly owned—that industry, the basis of our social life, instead of being the private property of the few and operated for their enrichment, ought to be the common property of all, democratically administered in the interest of all. . . .

I am opposing a social order in which it is possible for one man who does absolutely nothing that is useful to amass a fortune of hundreds of millions of dollars, while millions of men and women who work all the days of their lives secure barely enough for a wretched existence.

This order of things cannot always endure. I have registered my protest against it. I recognize the feebleness of my effort, but, fortunately, I am not alone. There are multiplied thousands of others who, like myself, have come to realize that before we may truly enjoy the blessings of civilized life, we must reorganize society upon a mutual and cooperative basis; and to this end we have organized a great economic and political movement that spreads over the face of all the earth.

There are today upwards of sixty millions of Socialists, loyal, devoted adherents to this cause, regardless of nationality, race, creed, color, or sex. They are all making common cause. They are spreading with tireless energy the propaganda of the new social order. They are waiting, watching, and working hopefully through all the hours of the day and the night. They are still in a minority. But they have learned how to be patient and to bide their time. They feel—they know, indeed—that the time is coming, in spite of all opposition, all persecution, when this emancipating gospel will spread among all the peoples, and when this minority will become the triumphant majority and, sweeping into power, inaugurate the greatest social and economic change in history.

In that day we shall have the universal commonwealth—the harmonious cooperation of every nation with every other nation on earth. . . .

Your Honor, I ask no mercy and I plead for no immunity. I realize that finally the right must prevail. I never so clearly comprehended as now the great struggle between the powers of greed and exploitation on the one hand and upon the other the rising hosts of industrial freedom and social justice.

I can see the dawn of the better day for humanity. The people are awakening. In due time they will and must come to their own.

"When the mariner, sailing over tropic seas, looks for relief from his weary watch, he turns his eyes toward the southern cross, burning luridly above the tempest-vexed ocean. As the midnight approaches, the southern cross begins to bend, the whirling worlds change their places, and with starry finger-points the Almighty marks the passage of time upon the dial of the universe, and though no bell may beat the glad tidings, the lookout knows that the midnight is passing and that relief and rest are close at hand.

Let the people everywhere take heart of hope, for the cross is bending, the midnight is passing, and joy cometh with the morning.

He's true to God who's true to man; wherever wrong is done,
To the humblest and the weakest, 'neath the all-beholding sun.
That wrong is done to us, and they are slaves most base,
Whose love of right is for themselves and not for all the race.

I am now prepared to receive your sentence.

8

Debs on Bolshevism
and International Revolution

*Debs revealed that he had the utmost sympathy for
the revolutionary leaders of wartime Russia and Germany. Like
the revolutionary European Spartacists in Germany and the Bolsheviks in Russia, Debs despised the moderate socialists as men
who preferred maintenance of capitalism to real social revolution. Hence Debs welcomed the Bolshevik Revolution and remained its staunch defender until his death. This did not stop
him from developing a position of critical support. After the
arrest of opposition Social Revolutionary leaders by the Bolsheviks in 1922, Debs wired Lenin to protest their planned execution,
and he admonished the Bolsheviks to "set an example" by upholding "the higher standards we seek to erect and profess to
observe."*

THE DAY OF THE PEOPLE [1]

Upon his release from the Kaiser's bastille—the doors of which
were torn from their hinges by the proletarian revolution—Karl
Liebknecht, heroic leader of the rising hosts, exclaimed: "The Day
of the People has arrived!" It was a magnificent challenge to the
Junkers and an inspiring battle-cry to the aroused workers.

From that day to this Liebknecht, Rosa Luxemburg, and other true
leaders of the German proletariat have stood bravely at the front, appealing to the workers to join the revolution and make it complete by
destroying what remained of the criminal and corrupt old regime and
ushering in the day of the people. Then arose the cry that the people
were not yet ready for their day, and Ebert and Scheidemann and
their crowd of white-livered reactionaries, with the sanction and support of the fugitive Kaiser, the infamous Junkers, and all the Allied
powers, now in beautiful alliance, proceeded to prove that the people were not yet ready to rule themselves by setting up a bourgeois
government under which the working class should remain in sub-

[1] *The Class Struggle*, February, 1919.

stantially the same state of slavish subjection they were in at the beginning of the war.

And now upon that issue—as to whether the terrible war has brought the people their day or whether its appalling sacrifices have all been in vain—the battle is raging in Germany as in Russia, and the near future will determine whether revolution has for once been really triumphant or whether sudden reaction has again won the day.

In the struggle in Russia the revolution has thus far triumphed for the reason that it has not compromised. The career of Kerensky was cut short when he attempted to turn the revolutionary tide into reactionary bourgeois channels.

Lenin and Trotzky were the men of the hour and under their fearless, incorruptible, and uncompromising leadership the Russian proletariat has held the fort against the combined assaults of all the ruling class powers of earth. It is a magnificent spectacle. It stirs the blood and warms the heart of every revolutionist, and it challenges the admiration of all the world.

So far as the Russian proletariat is concerned, the day of the people has arrived, and they are fighting and dying as only heroes and martyrs can fight and die to usher in the day of the people not only in Russia but in all the nations on the globe.

In every revolution of the past the false and cowardly plea that the people were "not yet ready" has prevailed. Some intermediate class invariably supplanted the class that was overthrown and "the people" remained at the bottom where they have been since the beginning of history. They have never been "ready" to rid themselves of their despots, robbers, and parasites. All they have ever been ready for has been to exchange one brood of vampires for another to drain their veins and fatten in their misery.

That was Kerensky's doctrine in Russia and it is Scheidemann's doctrine in Germany. They are both false prophets of the people and traitors to the working class, and woe be to their deluded followers if their vicious reaction triumphs, for then indeed will the yokes be fastened afresh upon their scarred and bleeding necks for another generation.

When Kerensky attempted to sidetrack the revolution in Russia by joining forces with the bourgeoisie he was lauded by the capitalist press of the whole world. When Scheidemann patriotically rushed to the support of the Kaiser and the Junkers at the beginning of the war, the same press denounced him as the betrayer of Socialism and the enemy of the people. And now this very press lauds him to the heavens as the savior of the German nation! Think of it! Scheidemann the traitor has become Scheidemann the hero of the bourgeoisie. Could it be for any other reason on earth than that Scheidemann is doing the dirty work of the capitalist class?

And all this time the prostitute press of the robber régime of the whole world is shrieking hideously against Bolshevism. "It is worse than Kaiserism" is the burden of their cry. Certainly it is. They would a thousand times rather have the Kaiser restored to his throne than to see the working class rise to power. In the latter event they cease to rule, their graft is gone and their class disappears, and well do they know it. That is what we said from the beginning and for which we have been sentenced as disloyalists and traitors.

Scheidemann and his breed do not believe that the day of the people has arrived. According to them the war and the revolution have brought the day of the bourgeoisie. Mr. Bourgeois is now to take the place of Mr. Junker—to evolute into another Junker himself by and by—while Mr. Wage-Slave remains where he was before, under the heels of his master, and all he gets out of the carnage in which his blood dyed the whole earth is a new set of heels to grind into his exploited bones and a fresh and lusty vampire to drain his life-blood.

Away with all such perfidious doctrines; forever away with such a vicious subterfuge and treacherous betrayal!

The people *are* ready for their day. *THE PEOPLE,* I say. Yes, *the people!*

Who are the people? The people are the working class, the lower class, the robbed, the oppressed, the impoverished, the great majority of the earth. They and those who sympathize with them are THE PEOPLE, and they who exploit the working class, and the mercenaries and menials who aid and abet the exploiters, are the enemies of the people.

That is the attitude of Lenin and Trotzky in Russia and was of Liebknecht and Rosa Luxemburg in Germany, and this accounts for the flood of falsehood and calumny which poured upon the heads of the brave leaders and their revolutionary movement from the filthy mouthpieces of the robber régime of criminal capitalism throughout the world.

The rise of the working class is the red specter in the bourgeois horizon. The red cock shall never crow. Anything but that! The Kaiser himself will be pitied and forgiven if he will but roll his eyes heavenward, proclaim the menace of Bolshevism, and appeal to humanity to rise in its wrath and stamp out this curse to civilization.

And still the "curse" continues to spread—like a raging conflagration it leaps from shore to shore. The reign of capitalism and militarism has made of all peoples inflammable material. They are ripe and ready for the change, the great change which means the rise and triumph of the workers, and end of exploitation, of war and plunder, and the emancipation of the race. Let it come! Let us all help its coming and pave the way for it by organizing the workers industrially and politically to conquer capitalism and usher in the day of the people.

In Russia and Germany our valiant comrades are leading the proletarian revolution, which knows no race, no color, no sex, and no boundary lines. They are setting the heroic example for world-wide emulation. Let us, like them, scorn and repudiate the cowardly compromisers within our own ranks, challenge and defy the robber-class power, and fight it out on that line to victory or death!

From the crown of my head to the soles of my feet I am Bolshevik, and proud of it.

"The Day of the People has arrived!"

PART TWO

DEBS VIEWED BY HIS CONTEMPORARIES

Debs as Humanist: His Friends and Neighbors Testify as to his Character

Eugene V. Debs grew up in Terre Haute, Indiana, a typical small midwestern town. Debs first entered union activity as a leader of the respectable Brotherhood of Locomotive Firemen. In his mid-20's, he had also been City Clerk. The respect and esteem which the local people had for Debs did not disappear. Although most of the town dwellers did not become radicals, their regard for Debs increased after he had become a prominent Socialist leader. To writers and lawyers, to union leaders, and even to Terre Haute's mayor, Debs remained Terre Haute's first citizen.[1]

CLARENCE A. ROYSE, ATTORNEY-AT-LAW

It has been my pleasure and privilege for a number of years to know well 'Gene Debs, to feel the glory and enthusiasm which radiates from his great soul, and to count his friendship among the blessings of a lifetime. As a champion of revolutionary political and social ideas, he naturally is misunderstood and reviled. In the minds of many people, his tall, gaunt, wiry figure stands as the embodiment of the spirit of hatred and envy, as a scourge going up and down the countless lighting [of] the fires of destruction. The utter falsity of this notion is apparent the moment one comes in personal contact with the man. I will not here discuss the validity of his political philosophy, or the worth of his social message, concerning which honest men may differ according to their several points of view, but will only suggest the quality of the man.

[1] From J. H. Hollingsworth, *Eugene V. Debs—What His Neighbors Say of Him* (Terre Haute, Indiana, 1916).

I venture to say that no one can really know 'Gene Debs and watch the kindly smile perpetually playing over his features, without perceiving that the basic motive of his character is love; an all embracing passionate sympathy, which demands for every fellow creature, a more abundant life. The earnestness and intensity of the man light up his features and crowd from his lips a rushing torrent of facts and ideas, illustrations and arguments. His eyes are aflame and to his finger tips he is alive.

'Gene Debs is one of those rare souls who are capable of a conviction so deep, a devotion so complete, as to centralize and unify every activity and interest of their lives. With him, personal ambitions, the attractions of money and possessions, ease and success, play no part. Abuse and appreciation are equally unimportant; he has no time for self-consciousness of any sort. That his message should get itself uttered is the one thing worthwhile for him, and to that work he gives himself joyfully and completely.

Equally he has in his heart no trace of resentment against any man or class of men. His fierce philipics are never uttered against persons, but only against injustice, ignorance, and oppression. He regards the degenerate beneficiaries of privilege as victims of the system, just as truly as are the exploited masses. He rejoices in all that man has achieved in material and mental possessions, and in the multiplied wealth that has come from scientific progress and industrial organization. He would hold fast all that is good, but his doctrine is that material things are good only as they minister to the souls of men. His voice rings out with an eloquence born of a deep conviction—a conviction of the injustice and stupid disorder of our industrial arrangements, whereby wealth accumulates and men decay. His concern is for men as human beings, each endowed with infinite possibilities of perfection. He would open to every creature the door of hope and opportunity, and remove the possibility of any man rising on the bruised bodies of his fellows. His motive power is the same religious zeal that inspired St. Francis—the gospel of the brotherhood of man.

Nevertheless, he is a wholly different type of man. He is absolutely modern and wholly human. He is of the twentieth century, or the twenty-first, and his eyes are set toward the future. The purpose he has in mind is the universal recognition of the fact that man is a social creature, that therefore altruism and egoism are one; that the welfare and destiny of each individual cell in the body politic, is inherently and necessarily bound up with the welfare and destiny of the organism. The means on which he relies are education, democracy, and the ballot, the awakening intelligence of the working class, and the consequent perfection of human institutions so as to fit human needs.

Although the most serious of men, he shows no trace of hardness, pessimism or austerity. He is a perpetual fountain of good cheer and good will. His heart leaps up when he beholds a rainbow in the sky, and to him the sky is ever aglow with the bright colors of hope. His interest in the ideas and activities of others is intense, his curiosity is insatiable, his joy in human fellowship is genuine, his fund of energy is inexhaustible. I have never known a more genial, lovable and radiant man than 'Gene Debs. He is one of the world's great men, and after the heat of contemporary political passions has cooled, he will inevitably take his true place on the roll of fame, as one who loved his fellow men, and as a powerful teacher and preacher of a new ideal of social justice.'

ROBERT HUNTER, WRITER

I remember as a little lad of eight or nine years, walking with my father in one of the streets of Terre Haute. A tall, slender, handsome young man stopped to talk with my father. At first I was fascinated by the way they grasped hands and looked into each other's eyes. I was then impressed by their animated conversation. But they talked on and on until it seemed to me hours in length; and finally I began to tug at my father's coattails, urging him to come on. After a while they parted, and my father said to me very seriously, "You should not interrupt me, Robert, when I am talking. That young man is one of the greatest souls on this earth, and you should have listened to what he said."

From time to time afterward I heard of 'Gene, and many were the stories told of him. Everyone spoke of his friendship for the poor. He could not keep money in his pocket. His wife says he always gives away his clothes to those who come to his door; and he gives his best suits, never his old ones.

Once I was told he had a gold watch of considerable value which had been given to him, and a fireman who had been out of work for some time stopped to say that he had a job offered him on the railroad, but he would have to have a watch before he could go to work. Immediately 'Gene took out his gold watch and gave it to the man, telling him to return it when he was able to buy one for himself.

These and countless other stories are told by his fellow citizens. Many of them do not understand 'Gene. His views and his work they cannot comprehend, but every man, woman, and child in that town loves him with a devotion quite extraordinary.

They say that a prophet is without honor in his own country, but in Terre Haute you will find that however much they misunderstand the work that 'Gene is doing there is not one who does not honor and love him.

Ask anyone. Go to the poor, the vagrant, the hobo. Go to the churches, to the rich, to the banker, to the traction magnate. You will find that every single one will say that 'Gene has something which other men do not possess. Some will say he is rash, unwise, and too radical. Others will say that he is too good for this world, and that his visions and dreams are the fanciful outpourings of a generous but impractical soul. But ask them about his character, his honesty, his sincerity, and unconsciously many of them will remove their hats.

Some of these statements will seem an exaggeration. But one cannot avoid that in speaking of 'Gene. When one who knows him makes any statement, no matter how moderate, it will seem to others who do not know him an exaggeration.

'Gene has followed Truth wherever she has led. He does not ask what is politic, what is wise, what is expedient; he only asks what is truth: He loves Truth beyond all things. She is his absolute mistress, and he has gone with her from riches to poverty, from popularity to unpopularity. He has gone with her out of great positions into small positions. He has stood up for her against all men. For her he has seemed at times to sacrifice all earthly gain and to accept without one pang of regret misunderstanding, misrepresentation, and almost universal condemnation. For her he has been momentarily one of the most popular men in the country and for her he has been momentarily one of the most unpopular men in the country. He has been her companion when everyone believed in her, and he has been her companion when to believe in her meant to go into prison stripes, behind iron bars.

Sometimes I have differed with 'Gene. I have said to him that what he was doing was unwise, impolitic, dangerous. At such times, under such criticism, he is always kindly, but undeterred; and it is his conscience that answers you back and asks, "But is it right? Is it true?"

Shortly after I left college I went to live in one of the most poverty-stricken districts of Chicago. One Sunday it was announced that Eugene would come there to speak. Thousands came to hear him, and overflowing the hall a multitude waited outside to hear him speak from a truck. After we had been waiting for two hours perhaps, 'Gene came out and began to speak. Most of the audience were foreigners who could hardly understand a word of English, and as I heard his beautiful words and saw their wistful earnest faces I felt that something more powerful, penetrating, and articulate than mere words was passing between the audience and the speaker. For a moment it seemed to me that a soul was speaking from the eyes and frame of 'Gene, and that, regardless of difference of language and all the traditional barriers that separated him from the multitude about him, they understood and believed all he said. I remember how my heart beat and how tears began to flow from my boyish eyes. I was ashamed for fear some one would see me. And it was not because of anything that 'Gene was saying. It was solely because of something back of the man, something greater than the man, something bigger, more powerful, and more moving than any words or expression. And after the thing was over I went to him, helped him on with his coat, and fondled him as I would my own brother. And as we went away together there kept coming into my heart the words of Ruth:

> Entreat me not to leave thee or to return from following after thee. For whither thou goest I will go, and whither thou lodgest I will lodge. Thy people shall be my people, and thy God my God.

JAMES LYONS, MAYOR OF TERRE HAUTE

EXECUTIVE DEPARTMENT
City of Terre Haute, Indiana
James Lyons, Mayor

February 27, 1907

John Cuthbertson,
  Crooked Lake, Michigan

Dear Sir: Yours of the 24th inst., requesting information without any political bias as to the standing of Eugene V. Debs in this community. In reply will state that while the overwhelming majority of the people here are opposed to the social and economic theories of Mr. Debs, that there is not, perhaps, a single man in this city who enjoys to a greater degree than Mr. Debs, the affection, love, and profound respect of the entire community. He is cultured, brilliant, eloquent, scholarly, companionable, and lovable in his relations with his fellowman. At home he is known as "Gene," and that perhaps indicates our feeling towards him as a man, independent of his political views. He numbers his friends and associates among all classes, rich and poor, and some of the richest men here, people who by very instinct are bitter against Socialism, are warm personal friends of Mr. Debs. His personal life is spotless and he enjoys a beautiful home life. Few public men have been more persistently and cruelly misrepresented by the press of the country. When such a man as James Whitcomb Riley, the Hoosier Poet, comes to Terre Haute, he is always the guest of Mr. Debs.

If you care to use this letter in any way for publication you are at liberty to do so. Every word I have written, and I am not in sympathy with Mr. Debs' views on Socialism, I know would be heartily indorsed by the people of this city.

Very respectfully,
James Lyons, Mayor

PHIL K. REINBOLD, LOCAL UNION LEADER

For several years past a report has been persistently circulated, with malice aforethought, to the effect that the house that Eugene V. Debs lives in was built by nonunion labor, that it was painted by non-union labor, and kept in repair by nonunion labor.

This report was first sprung in the presidential campaign of 1908 and at that time telegraphed over all the country to injure Debs's candidacy; it was revived in the campaign of 1912 and it has been given a fresh start since his recent indictment in the federal court.

Sometimes this report appears in one form and sometimes another, but however it may vary, its object is always the same and that is to discredit Debs in the eyes of union men.

The undersigned, who has lived in the same town with Debs and has known him intimately during the last twenty-seven years, having been active in union labor during all that time, now issues this statement to deny the reports above mentioned as being absolutely false and as having no shadow of foundation in fact.

These reports have but one purpose and that is not to help union labor but to hurt Debs who has worked all his life to make union labor what it is today. As nothing that is true of him can be sprung to hurt Debs, resort must be had to falsehood and slander and that is the object of these malicious and lying reports which are frequently brought to my attention and which I now deny publicly in the interest of truth and justice.

The fact is that Debs organized most of the unions in this city and when he was grand secretary and treasurer of the Brotherhood of Locomotive Firemen his office was headquarters for organized labor unions of every kind and form. When unions needed money they went to Debs; when they were in trouble they went to Debs; when they had grievances they went to Debs. It was Debs who arbitrated all their early troubles or led their strikes over and over again, and never once did he turn his back on a labor union or a union man.

This is but a small part of his record as a union man here in Terre Haute where we have been in close touch with him for over a quarter of a century and know him for what he is.

I ask every union paper in the interest of common justice to publish this statement and help to stamp out this infamous lie. No one who utters it will dare to face the undersigned in doing so, or any other union man here in Terre Haute where the facts are known.

It is very easy to understand why Wall Street capitalists should circulate this and other slanders about Debs, but certainly no true union workingman will give them currency.

Phil K. Reinbold
President, Central Labor Union

Terre Haute, Ind., Feb. 22, 1913

J. P. MAC DONAGH, TYPOGRAPHER

Editor National Rip-Saw:

Sir:—In a recent issue of your widely circulated paper I noted that Eugene V. Debs was compelled to stoop to the humiliating position of defending himself from the cowardly, scurrilous attack made upon him by a fellow named Grant Hamilton of Salt Lake City, while there in the capacity of paid organizer for the American Federation of Labor. It appears that this blatant fakir tried to convey the impression that Debs, "while editor of the Locomotive Firemen's Magazine, had the printing done in a nonunion office, and that when a committee from the Typographical Union called upon him to protest that he (Debs) ordered them from his office."

In answer to this cowardly charge I want to say that when Hamilton made it he lied, damnably lied, and had I been president I would have forced that lie down his sordid throat when his foul tongue uttered it.

I was President of the Terre Haute Typographical Union No. 76, when "Our Gene," as we lovingly called the great humanitarian, had charge of the publication of the Locomotive Firemen's Magazine, and can vouch for the fact that the firm of Moore & Langen, where he had his printing done, was strictly a union shop and that Debs was the man who made it so. That firm had to furnish Debs with the printers' union label, the insignia of our craft, or they never would have been allowed to do the work. No, not by Debs, and the idea of a committee of the printers' union waiting on him with a protest is not only false and slanderous but utterly absurd.

Eugene V. Debs is on the roster—or should be—as honorary member of Terre Haute Typographical Union No. 76 for the manifold

good offices he rendered the union, and when his name was presented
for that honor there was not a dissenting voice, and when I, as presi-
dent of the union, put the motion to the members it was carried
unanimously.

Well do I remember the long and bitter fight we printers had with
the nonunion Gazette at Terre Haute, and with the aid of the other
unions we almost had that sheet call "30" on its existence. Then it
was that the labor crushers, the rich republicans composed of con-
tractors, builders, and manufacturers, came to the aid of the Ball
brothers, its publishers, and pledged their money and influence (although the Gazette was the official democratic organ of Vigo County),
providing they would continue fighting the trade unions until they
were wiped out of existence. This infused new life in the Gazette,
and the unions soon began to feel the pressure and the persecution.
The intention of the labor crushers, now all combined, would soon
have been accomplished had not "Our Gene" come to the rescue by
enlisting a few good Samaritans who, with himself, put up the money,
purchased a printing plant and launched "The Evening News," which
soon gained a large circulation among workingmen. But, alas! It was
doomed to be driven out of existence and after two years of useful
service suspended publication. This was brought about by its enemies,
who, working secretly for its destruction, in some mysterious way
foisted a fellow named Connor on the paper who was entrusted with
its business management, and he soon completed his dastardly work.
This fellow, smooth as a Judas, inquisitive as a spy, and crafty as a
Pinkerton hireling, in a few short months put the paper on the rocks
and then suddenly departed, leaving the printers with some $50 to
$100 coming to them for back salary and a lot of other unsettled bills.
    Debs and his associates who originally financed the project did all
in their power to resuscitate the paper, but in vain. They were out
their original investment for the plant and could not raise sufficient
capital to resume publication, but Brother Debs raised many a dollar
for those who suffered the loss of their salary, and helped others get
situations in other industries.
    If I were to recount one-half the good offices Eugene V. Debs did
for the trade unions while I was in Terre Haute, I could fill up the
entire pages of The Rip-Saw, and then a supplement would have to
be added. Suffice it to say that he helped the writer to organize many
of the trade unions of Terre Haute in those days, and many a night
did we rouse him out of his bed to come and help settle some dispute
or other between employer and employees, for the printers, the
painters, the lathers and plasterers, the coopers, the cigar makers, the

carpenters, the brick makers, the hodcarriers, and many others which I have borne witness to.

Believe me, Mr. Editor, it would not be healthy for Hamilton to express himself about Eugene V. Debs in Terre Haute as he did in Salt Lake City, No! Instead of escaping what he deserved for his cowardly utterance—a bath in Salt Lake—he assuredly would not escape a dip in the Wabash before leaving the Prairie City.

Debs, for his sincere honesty of purpose, his genial, warmhearted disposition, his faithful, untiring efforts to uplift the downtrodden, is loved by the union men, revered by those who do not agree with him politically, and respected by all who know him. The true character of this great man is summed up by James Whitcomb Riley, the "Hoosier poet," in his dialect poem, "Regardin' Terre Haute":

> And there's 'Gene Debs—a man 'at stands
> And just holds out in his two hands
> As warm a heart as ever beat
> Betwixt here and the Jedgement Seat!

J. P. MacDonagh
845 Grant St., Akron, Ohio

May 10th, 1914

Elizabeth Gurley Flynn: A Remembrance of an IWW Leader

When she wrote her account of Debs in 1939, Elizabeth Gurley Flynn had become a leading American Communist. This position colored her account of Debs, since she sought to assess his strengths and weaknesses according to party doctrine. But her account is based on Gurley Flynn's acquaintance with Debs when she was a fighter in the IWW, and it is in this regard that her piece has historic merit.[1]

> *One of the best loved leaders of the American proletariat, Eugene V. Debs. I am not surprised that this fearless man was thrown in prison by the American bourgeoisie.*
>
> —V. I. LENIN

To hear Eugene V. Debs speak on any occasion was an unforgettable experience. He was a matchless orator. No one who heard Debs came away entirely unaffected. People who came merely from curiosity were held spellbound by his torrent of burning eloquence. He exemplified Wendell Phillips' advice on how to be a speaker, "Be so full of your subject that you flow over like a pitcher!" Debs paced back and forth on the platform, like a lion ready to spring, then leaned far over the edge, his tall gaunt frame bending like a reed, his long bony finger pointing—his favorite gesture. His deep blue eyes appeared to look searchingly at each one in the audience, he seemed to be speaking directly to each individual. Such intimate eloquence is hardly possible in this era of mechanized speech. Debs's voice was strong and clear and could be heard in the largest hall and outdoor places. He spoke with imagery and poetry of expression, drew word pictures of the lives of the workers, of child labor, of men in prison, or at war. He was full of loving kindness of those who are heavily laden, and had a searing contempt for "gory-beaked vultures" who fatten on their exploitation.

[1] From "Eugene V. Debs," in Elizabeth Gurley Flynn, *Debs, Haywood, Ruthenberg* (New York, 1939), 11–19. Reprinted by permission of International Publishers Co., Inc.

His strong sense of labor solidarity never wavered. He responded to appeals from the most obscure workers.

I met him in the small town of Minersville, Pa., where we spoke together, on an old wagon, to the daughters of the miners who were engaged in a textile strike. He had been lecturing in the state. We telegraphed asking him to come to encourage the strikers, hardly expecting him, as we were quite far away. I have a precious snapshot of 'Gene Debs leaning eagerly out over the tail of the wagon in his characteristic pose, smiling encouragement to those young girl strikers. No audience in a great auditorium of a metropolitan city heard a more beautiful and moving speech than 'Gene Debs delivered that day thirty years ago in the Anthracite

He was *an agitator,* born of the first national awakening of American labor. The shame of servitude and the glory of struggle were emblazoned in the mind of every worker who heard Debs. The first definition of agitator was given when Pontius Pilate called for the accusation against "this just man" and the bloodthirsty howl went up: "Crucify him—he stirreth up the people!" Debs did stir the people, because of his deep roots in them.

When he was twenty. Debs became a charter member of a trade union, the Brotherhood of Locomotive Firemen, and was made Secretary of the Terre Haute local. Old Josh Leach, the founder of the Brotherhood, remarked in St. Louis a few days after, "I put a towheaded boy in the Brotherhood in Terre Haute not long ago, and some day he will be at the head of it." One of the few boasts Debs made was that he never missed a union meeting in ten years. In 1880, when he was twenty-five, he became General Secretary-Treasurer of the national union. . . .

The nationwide railroad strike of the late seventies particularly affected the Middle West. This spurred him to organize not only his own craft but all others on the roads. His union, which had sixty lodges and a $6,000 debt when he started, soon had 226 lodges and no debts. He organized brakemen, switchmen, telegraphers, shopmen, trackmen. In 1893 he organized the first industrial union of railroad workers in this country, the American Railway Union.

He gave up his $4,000 a year salary with the Brotherhood of Locomotive Firemen to work for $75 a month for the "unification of all railroad employees for their mutual benefit and protection." The new organization successfully won a struggle on the Great Northern Railroad—97½ percent of their demands—a monthly increase of $14,000 in wages.

In 1894, the American Railway Union entered into a life and death conflict—a sympathetic strike in defense of the Pullman Company shop workers who struck against a wage cut. Federal troops were sent in by

President Cleveland to break the strike, over the protest of Governor Altgeld of Illinois. Sweeping injunctions were issued by the federal courts. Debs and the other strike leaders were arrested. They were held in the old Cook County Jail, in Chicago, now happily torn down. Charges of conspiracy, treason, and murder simmered down to violating the injunctions.

Debs served six months in Woodstock County Jail. Here, he says "Socialism gradually laid hold of me in its own irresistible fashion." A volume of Marx's *Capital* and other Socialist books were brought to him in jail. Debs was never antipolitical, although then he was absorbed in union affairs. He had been City Clerk of Terre Haute for four years, elected on the Democratic ticket, and a member of the Indiana legislature in 1885. The defeat of the ARU by troops, courts, and the 3,600 United States deputy marshals (who rode the trains to "protect the mails") marked the beginning of Debs as a Socialist leader. "I was baptized in socialism, in the roar of the conflict," he said. He devoted the balance of his life to it.

He served as a special organizer in 1897, in the West for both the United Mine Workers and the Western Federation of Miners. After that he concentrated on politics. He organized the Social-Democracy of America in 1897. In 1900 this group joined with a section which split away from the Socialist Labor party, and formed the Socialist party. Debs was the presidential standard bearer of the Socialist party in five campaigns from 1900 to 1920. In 1920 he polled 920,000 votes while "silenced" in Atlanta Penitentiary.

When Debs declined to run in 1916, the S.P. lost over 300,000 votes, which indicates that Debs was the natural leader of the party. Yet the party officials deliberately isolated him. They created the impression that Debs was only a great heart and voice but that they were the brains. Such was not the case. It was because he took a more advanced position on trade-union work, working-class political action, immigration, labor defense, the war, the Russian Revolution, and the Soviet government. Alexander Trachtenberg, speaking from twenty years' personal observation, says:

> On many occasions Debs was in open conflict with the S.P. leadership. Although considered as such, Debs really was never the political leader of the party. He represented perhaps the greatest peculiarity in the American Socialist movement. Considered by the rank and file as the personification of the fighting spirit of socialism and looked upon by the outside world as the outstanding personality in the American Socialist movement, Debs never wrote a platform for the party, never sat on its executive committee, except or the last two or three years of his life when he was brought in more for window dressing, never was sent as a delegate to a national or international convention, never

was permitted to participate in the councils of the party to formulate policies and work out tactics. The leadership of the S.P. studiously avoided bringing Debs into the organization. He was kept on the platform where his eloquence was capitalized, or he was allowed to write in fugitive and privately owned Socialist journals rather than in the official organs of the party.

The S.P. leadership feared Deb's revolutionary attitude on the burning questions which agitated the membership of the party. . . . Debs should have never permitted himself to be placed in such a position by the S.P. leaders. His place was among the proletarian members, guarding the party against the reformist leaders and guiding the membership in his own spirit of militancy. *He should have been the political leader of the party* instead of letting that leadership fall into the hands of lawyers and ministers." *

Like a caged lion, he roared occasionally at his role as a captive celebrity. On several historic issues he broke loose. So today workers remember Debs while those who tried to hold his mighty spirit in leash are forgotten. Debs was a logical forerunner of the Communist party.

In an article "Danger Ahead" (1911) Debs warned against the party losing its working-class character. He objected (1910) to the party accepting the American Federation of Labor policy of excluding immigrants; he was a signer of the IWW manifesto (1905) and advocated organizing the unorganized when the S.P. official position was "neutrality" on the trade unions. He advocated industrial unionism and opposed kowtowing to the reactionary American Federation of Labor craft leaders. He pointed out that *"No politics in the unions"* was a farce, that Gompers was not opposed to politics (he was a master at the game), but to independent working-class political action.

Sometimes Debs was confused theoretically but he could be depended upon in all major issues, guided instinctively by his class consciousness. In 1907, thirty years after their execution, when the name of the "Molly Maguires" was still spoken in whispers, Debs wrote of them as "the first martyrs to the class struggle in the United States."

He wrote of the Haymarket martyrs of 1887, "these leaders of labor paid the penalty of their loyalty. This judicial massacre constitutes the blackest page in American history!"

His famous editorial "Arouse Ye Slaves!" in the *Appeal to Reason* on March 10, 1906, was a call to action for Moyer, Haywood, Pettibone, who were accused of murder in Idaho.

"If the plutocrats begin the program we will finish it!" he cried, to the horror of his pussyfooting advisers. He passionately defended Mooney and Billings, Joe Hill, the IWW, Sacco and Vanzetti.

* Introduction to *Speeches of Eugene V. Debs,* p. 14, International Publishers, New York.

The speech which he made in Canton, Ohio, on June 16, 1918, during the First World War, in defense of Charles E. Ruthenberg, Alfred Wagenknecht, and Charles Baker resulted in his arrest on the charge of violating the Espionage Act. He had just visited his imprisoned comrades in the nearby jail. He said "I am proud of them. They are there for us and we are here for them." He reiterated his opposition to the capitalists' war. He was guided by the principles of international socialism. *Debs was not a pacifist.* He said clearly:

> No, I am not opposed to fighting under all circumstances, and any declaration to the contrary would disqualify me as a revolutionist. . . . I am opposed to every war but one; I am for that war with heart and soul and that is the world-wide war of the social revolution.

He said further:

> While I have not a drop of blood to shed for the oppressors of the working class and the robbers of the poor, the thieves and looters, the brigands and murderers, whose debauched misrule is the crime of the ages, I have a heart full to shed for their victims when it shall be needed in the war for their liberation.

This, he believed, "is where the Socialist party ought to stand on war." He gave his great heart fearlessly. He addressed the world, through the jury, for two hours on September 12, 1918, was found guilty and sentenced to ten years. When his sentence was affirmed by the U.S. Supreme Court he said:

> I have no concern with what a coterie of begowned corporation lawyers in Washington may decide. The court of final resort is the people, and that court will be heard from in due time.

At the age of 65, five months after the Armistice was signed, and in delicate health, he was sent to prison in Moundsville, West Virginia. He was removed to Atlanta Penitentiary because there were fears that he would be liberated by the miners of the area. On entering prison, he said, "I enter the prison doors a flaming revolutionist—my head erect, my spirit untamed, and my soul unconquerable!" He was in prison for over two years, was finally pardoned by President Harding but without restoration of citizenship.

The left-wing split from the Socialist party and the organization of the Communist party took place while Debs was in prison. Possibly if Debs had been outside he would have left the party whose degeneration he had foreseen, and taken his place, where he logically belonged, with the left-wing forces who organized the Communist party.

The Russian Revolution was greeted by Debs as "the greatest in point of historic significance and far-reaching influence in the annals of the human race."

When he was nominated for the presidency in 1920 he told the Socialist Party Notification Committee who came to Atlanta, "I heartily support the Russian Revolution without reservations."

After his arrest, before his trial, he sent "Greetings to our Russian Comrades," on the occasion of the first anniversary of the revolution. On November 7, 1920, while he was in Atlanta Penitentiary, he wrote: "Greetings on the third anniversary of the Russian Revolution. The emancipation of Russia and the establishment of the Workers' Republic is an inspiration to the workers of the world." He explained: "There is no autocracy in the rule of the masses," even though he was not clear on Lenin's conception of the state and the *proletarian* dictatorship. He had the correct instinct to insist that: "During the revolutionary period, the revolution must protect itself."

Debs once wrote that: "The most heroic word in all languages is revolution." He wanted to be counted always as a revolutionist. He joined the Friends of the Soviet Union and the International Labor Defense when he came out of prison, in spite of the Socialist party boycott. Until his death he defended the Bolsheviks and the Soviet Union. He died October 20, 1926, after a long illness.

He did not consider himself a leader in a personal sense. He said:

> If you are looking for a Moses to lead you out of this capitalist wilderness you will stay right where you are. I would not lead you into the promised land if I could, because if *I* could lead you in, somebody else could lead you out. You must use your heads as well as your hands and get yourselves out of your present condition; as it is now, the capitalists use your heads and your hands.

We admire and love Eugene V. Debs, great agitator, and "American Bolshevik," as he so proudly called himself.

Emma Goldman:
An Anarchist View

Emma Goldman was America's most noted anarchist leader. A firm opponent of the Marxian socialists, she argued that the social revolution had to begin with destruction of the State machinery. Suspicious and wary of the political struggle waged by the Socialists, she nevertheless welcomed Debs as a comrade in the struggle. Debs's own nonsectation approach to various sectors of the Left is revealed in this document.[1] Although Emma Goldman tried to argue that Debs was indeed close to the anarchist, Debs's commitment to political action always remained prominent in his own political arsenal.

During my stay in Chicago I attended a labor convention in session in the city [1893]. I met a number of people there prominent in trade-union and revolutionary ranks. . . . The most striking figure at the convention was Eugene V. Debs. Very tall and lean, he stood out above his comrades in more than a physical sense; but what struck me most about him was his naive unawareness of the intrigues going on around him. Some of the delegates, nonpolitical socialists, had asked me to speak and had the chairman put me on the list. By obvious trickery the Social Democratic politicians succeeded in preventing my getting the floor. At the conclusion of the session Debs came over to me to explain that there had been an unfortunate misunderstanding, but that he and his comrades would have me address the delegates in the evening.

In the evening neither Debs nor the committee was present. The audience consisted of the delegates that had extended the invitation to me and of our own comrades. Debs arrived, all out of breath, almost at the close. He had tried to get away from the various sessions in order to hear me, he said, but he had been detained. Would I forgive him and take lunch with him the next day? I had the feeling that possibly he had been a party to the petty conspiracy to suppress me. At the same time I could not reconcile his frank and open demeanour

[1] From Emma Goldman, *Living My Life* (New York: Alfred A. Knopf, 1934), pp. 220–21. Copyright 1934 by Alfred A. Knopf, Inc., and reprinted with their permission.

with mean actions. I consented. After spending some time with him I was convinced that Debs was in no way to blame. Whatever the politicians in his party might be doing, I was sure that he was decent and high-minded. His belief in the people was very genuine, and his vision of socialism was quite unlike the State machine pictured in Marx's communist manifesto. Hearing his views, I could not help exclaiming: "Why, Mr. Debs, you're an anarchist!" "Not Mister, but Comrade," he corrected me; "won't you call me that?" Clasping my hand warmly, he assured me that he felt very close to the anarchists, that anarchism was the goal to strive for, and that all socialists should also be anarchists. Socialism to him was only a stepping-stone to the ultimate ideal, which was anarchism. "I know and love Kropotkin and his work," he said; "I admire him and I revere our murdered comrades who lie in Waldheim, as I do all the other splendid fighters in your movement. You see, then, I am your comrade. I am with you in your struggle." I pointed out that we could not hope to achieve freedom by increasing the power of the State, which the socialists were aiming at. I stressed the fact that political action is the death-knell of the economic struggle. Debs did not dispute me, agreeing that the revolutionary spirit must be kept alive notwithstanding any political objects, but he thought the latter a necessary and practical means of reaching the masses.

We parted good friends. Debs was so genial and charming as a human being that one did not mind the lack of political clarity which made him reach out at one and the same time for opposite poles.

Samuel Gompers: Debs, The Apostle of Failure[1]

An avowed opponent of the socialists in the ranks of organized labor, Samuel Gompers disliked Debs's commitment to industrial unionism as well. As chieftain of the American Federation of Labor, Gompers opted for organization of skilled labor within the existing political economy. His attitude toward employers was dictated by whether or not the employer would deal with the craft federation; size, power, and wealth of the corporation did not enter into consideration. Hence Gompers joined forces in 1900 with industrialist-politician Mark Hanna as co-chairman of the National Civic Federation, for the purpose of resolving class conflict and instituting cooperative relations between capital and labor. Unlike Debs, Gompers believed that industrial peace would reign, since the "men who control wealth in this country are at bottom human and adaptable to the changed order of relations."

So Debs has joined the mob of howling dervishes who are kicking up a great dust and trying to discourage the men in the labor movement from using their political power in conjunction with their industrial forces in order to protect the rights of the masses who toil. Abuse by Debs was to be expected. His past history is all in the direction of harming rather than helping the labor movement. His hostility would not be worthy of notice except for one thing. We especially desire to call attention to this because Debs's abuse is a type of what may be expected during the whole campaign. Compare anything Debs may say with the most virulent attacks upon Labor by the Parry-Post-Van Cleave gang.* Note the remarkable similarity between them—then it becomes an easy guess as to where Debs gets his inspiration, and possibly even his financial backing.

The attack by Debs is the more-despicable because he poses as a friend and representative of labor—even as a labor martyr forsooth!

[1] From *The American Federationist* (September, 1908), pp. 736–40. Reprinted by permission of the AFL-CIO *American Federationist*.

* Gompers refers to the leadership of the antiunion group among the National Association of Manufacturers.

His sort of attack is one of the insidious methods adopted by our opponents to disorganize the workers, lead them astray from the vital issues, and then corral their votes into some adjunct or side-light assistance to the Republican party, and thus by indirection defeat the efforts of the intelligent and patriotic workers.

Mr. Debs denounces all those who differ from him as tricksters, frauds, and fakirs. To listen to him it would appear that one Mr. Debs has the monopoly of all honesty and virtue. But we have met this sort of men before in the political and industrial arena. They usually are the incarnation of the abusive epithets which they so recklessly hurl at other people.

Now, pray, what has Debs ever done in the interest of labor? What has he ever said when he had the official opportunity to say the word in the interest of the working people? It is one thing to boast of what one is willing to do when one has not the opportunity, and quite another to fail to turn a hand to help when in position to do so.

Mr. Debs since he went to jail in the injunction case growing out of the American Railway Union strike has worn an illusory halo which no one has been desirous of disturbing. It pleases him. He wears it on all occasions and describes it with a heartrending, tear-shedding exhibition of emotion. But let us lift the curtain from the cant and hypocrisy of this heroic, self-sacrificing Mr. Debs. In what manner has he benefited by word or act the working people of this country?

We note the "Socialists' Special" train is to make a tour of the country, carrying Mr. Debs with all the luxurious accessories which modern transportation can accomplish. The train is said to cost $23,000 for the campaign. Now we would like to inquire who finances the Socialist campaign? It seems hardly probable that such luxurious style of transportation would be authorized by those voters of small means whose contributions are alleged to be the chief support of the Socialist campaign. Why not publish a list of your campaign contributions, Mr. Debs? It would be interesting to know who contributes the $23,000 campaign train. There is a strong suspicion in the minds of many that the money has the same similarity of source as the abuse. In other words, that the interests behind the Parry-Post-Van Cleave-Taft-Debs opposition to unions furnishes the money for any branch of the campaign where it is expected to do the most harm to the unions and their friends. Come out into the open, Mr. Debs. Where does your party get the money? What is the real reason of your virulent hostility to the American Federation of Labor political campaign?

A little history of Mr. Debs's vagaries may refresh the memory of our readers at this time and suggest the motive of the present hostility. For many years Mr. Debs was secretary of the Brotherhood of Locomotive Firemen and editor of its official magazine. During the major portion of that time no man in that organization had so much opportunity as he to sway the judgment and action of the membership of that organization in the right direction. Yet when or where did he say one word or perform one act wherein he showed his desire or advocated the proposition for the Brotherhood of Locomotive Firemen becoming part of the great body of organized workers of America? Yet this certainly would have been helpful by bringing them in closer touch with the mass of workers.

If he answers that he declined to advocate that course on account of, "Mr. Gompers being at the head of the American Federation of Labor," our rejoinder is that during 1895 Mr. Gompers was not the president of the American Federation of Labor and at that time had no notion of ever again becoming its president.

Mr. Debs set about to organize a rival to the Brotherhood of Locomotive Firemen and other railway organizations—the American Labor Union. He did this in the hope of helping the worst elements of the capitalist class to crush out not only the American Federation of Labor, but every other labor organization in the country. That he failed in misleading the workers and wrecking their organizations was due to no lack of effort on his part. He tried hard, as hard as any man with a bad cause could.

He organized the American Railway Union and became its president in rivalry to the organization whose official he still was. He hoped and worked and plotted for the destruction of the organization of which he was a responsible official.

When a large number of men in the American Railway Union responded to Mr. Debs's call to strike and many became blacklisted and victimized, he advocated and finally secured the abandonment of the American Railway Union, and thus left his men high and dry without the slightest organized protection.

When Mr. Debs realized the hopelessness of the American Railway Union strike, in desperation he brought every influence to bear to have the men in the bona fide labor movement to "order" a general strike of all the workers of our country—to plunge themselves into a contest which was a forlorn hope from the start.

While Mr. Debs was secretary of the Brotherhood of Locomotive Firemen and editor of its official magazine that organization held one of its conventions at Cincinnati. He had given the order for the convention printing to a concern which had a contest on with the Cincinnati Typographical Union. A committee of Cincinnati union printers called upon Mr. Debs to ask him to use the influence of his position to urge the printing company to come to an amicable adjustment with the union, or, failing in that, to give the convention printing to a union house. Did Mr. Debs comply with that request? Not a bit of it. He insulted the committee and told them he wanted nothing to do with them or their union.

The American Federation of Labor has always urged the moral obligation of all unions to be a part of the American Federation of Labor, the only federation of the workers which has proved its power and influence for good in the interests of labor and which is the first general organization or federation to have a long-continued beneficent period of existence. Whenever any effort was made by the American Federation of Labor to have a labor organization affiliate, Mr. Debs endeavored to be present and used every subterfuge and species of sophistry to prevent such a consummation, the last instance being his successful interference when Secretary Frank Morrison of the American Federation of Labor went to Denver to urge the Western Federation of Miners to resume its affiliation to the American Federation of Labor, the affiliation having been abandoned against the direct instruction of a general convention of that organization.

When Mr. Debs had about run to the end of his tether, when he launched and officered in turn the American Railway Union, the Western Labor Union, and the American Labor Union, which each in turn he wrecked, he then, in desperation, threw himself, body, boots, and breeches, into the Industrial (Wonder) Workers of the World and advocated the destruction of every trade and labor union, including the American Federation of Labor. When he had proved himself the Apostle of Failure in every industrial effort which he undertook, he finally launched another pet idea—none other than a land speculation colonization scheme which in his own good time he also abandoned.

When Mr. Debs was a candidate for the Indiana legislature, on which ticket did he run? On the Democratic.

In 1896 for which ticket and party did Mr. Debs stump the country? The Democratic. For which candidate did he urge the workers and the people generally to vote? Mr. Bryan.

As a matter of fact since Mr. Debs has been taking an active part in presidential campaigns he has advocated the election of the candidate of the Democratic party every time, except those campaigns when he himself was a candidate.

Mr. Debs asserts that "Gompers has always declared that politics must never be discussed in labor unions." In making this false assertion he has taken for granted the political party socialists' malicious misrepresentations of our men and our movement, and as usual Mr. Debs makes not the slightest effort to ascertain the facts.

We venture to assert that Mr. Debs will fail to find an authentic word uttered orally or in print where such a thought is advocated or expressed by the writer hereof. What has been urged, advocated, and insistently pressed is that the trade-union movement is higher, better, nobler, purer, and far more efficient to permanently conserve the interests of labor than any political party; that the trade unions are the only organizations instituted by, for, and directly governed by the wage-workers for their own protection and advancement.

We have said and repeat that the bona fide labor movement of our country is nonpartisan politically in the sense that, as a movement it is *above* and *better than political partisanship.*

Because Mr. Debs has had injunctions served upon him he imagines he understands the basis upon which they are issued and the contentions of labor against them. His entire discussion of the subject betrays a woeful ignorance. Many men have had surgical operations performed upon them without the slightest knowledge of medicine or surgery. Mr. Debs is as ignorant as a newborn babe of the underlying principles involved in the injunction abuse. And, indeed, he manifests no desire to learn.

We recognize that many men of labor, both members and nonmembers of unions, often differ in their political party affiliations. We know, too, that, despite this fact, the intelligent workers, the men who know the wrongs which they or their fellows have been compelled to endure, who know the rights to which they are justly entitled, who know that the Van Cleaves, Parrys, and Posts have conspired with the worst elements of the capitalists to rivet the chains of slavery upon them, to deprive them of the rights which are theirs—can and will prove themselves something more than political partisans. They will show that they are workers, wealth producers, men, citizens, Americans, and will unite in one common cause for the good of all.

Lincoln Steffens Learns about Debs and Socialism

Lincoln Steffens is widely regarded as one of the outstanding political journalists of the Progressive Era. Author of the heralded study of corruption in urban America, The Shame of the Cities, *Steffens was one of the luminaries in the group that Theodore Roosevelt dubbed as "muckrakers." Steffens was to grow more radical as the years passed. His long interview with Debs exemplified the respect with which Steffens looked at Debs and American socialism. Because of Steffens' skill as a writer, the interview provided rich insights into Debs's approach and thought.[1]*

All radicals have programs. They differ radically among themselves. They cannot, therefore, all have "the" program of God and man which each one thinks his is. Not one of them may be sound, reasonable, desirable, or right. They may all be impossible. But, at least, they are programs, not merely platforms. Therefore they concern us.

For we want to know what the causes are of our American corruption, and the cure. We have asked the leaders of the two old parties, and, excepting La Follette, they said, or they showed, that they didn't really know. Socialists, with other radicals, are sure they do know. So we will let them tell us what they think the matter is and what they think we ought to do about it.

The President, Taft, and John Johnson don't believe there is any "it"; they set aside the suggestion that most of our greater evils are traceable to a few fundamental, removable causes. There's the money question and the tariff issue; the regulation of railroads, trusts, and criminals. They recognize seriously, though separately, these problems of business and money. Not so the problems of men and women: labor, poverty, crime. As the old political parties of Europe did so long, ours deny or ignore the social problem. The Socialists (whence the name) not only recognize, they offer a solution for it. Therefore Socialism grows.

[1] From Lincoln Steffens, "Eugene V. Debs on What the Matter is in America and What To Do About It," *Everybody's* (October, 1908), pp. 455–69.

111

For there is a social problem, and men find it out. The schools
don't teach it; the churches don't preach it; the press won't mention
it; and, brought up, as we are, to mind our own business, we become
too absorbed in that to pay much attention to our public business.
But when the railroad magnate discovers that, to make his property
pay, he must corrupt politics, and that, having done so, he is first
honored, then disgraced, he learns that there is something wrong somewhere. And when the willing worker out of work sees the market
glutted with goods he and his family need but cannot buy, he, also,
realizes that there are problems of humanity, as well as of money, in
a money panic. The "bum," who is often an ex-child laborer, and
the shop-girl who ekes out a living by taking a "gentleman friend"—
they feel it vaguely. And I, going about from city to city and from
state to state, and finding everywhere much the same conditions,
due to essentially the same forces, operated by all sorts of men using
similar methods for one everlasting purpose and to one identical end,
I, slowly, reluctantly, am convinced that we all are facing some one
great common problem.

And we are. There is some relation between the unhappy capitalist
facing the prison bars and the miserable workman staring into the
shop window. There is some causal connection between the man and
the money that are out of employment. And the trust, the railroad
rebate, the bribed legislator, the red-light dive, and the working girl
gone wrong form a living chain that can, and shall, be broken.

This is the problem of society as a whole, and as men find it out
in fear and doubt, they look first to their old leaders; not for a final
solution; all they ask is some recognition of it, some word of interest,
comfort, hope. But when, seeing Congress passing an emergency currency bill to help money in distress, the unemployed assemble to ex-
hibit their needs and "are given the stick"; when, watching Capital
forming trusts and combines, labor organizes unions and, asking relief from a power the courts have abused, gets an ambiguous anti-
injunction plank; when, asking where they can find work, men hear
that "God knows"; then, slowly, reluctantly, but naturally, they turn
to the agitator on the street corner. He says he knows, and he makes
it all plain; too plain, perhaps; but at least he understands the troubles
of all those that are weary and heavy-laden, and he says he will give
them rest. Is it any wonder they go to him, as they do?

The Socialists more than double their number every four years in
the United States, and in Europe they did so till now they have in
every parliament a strong, disciplined, uncompromising minority
which seeks reform, not office; the Socialist leaders that have accepted
seats in cabinets have been read out of their party. No, this remarkable international organization stands there compact and keen, de-

manding, amending, debating, and reporting back to the people. And that counts. The Socialist party is dictating policies to all the first-class governments abroad. Holding up its own menacing program in one hand and pointing with the other at its ever-growing vote, it is compelling the old parties to attempt social, not alone financial and political, reforms.

"We had to take up social reforms," said the prime minister of England, Sir Henry Campbell-Bannerman, just before he died, to an American friend of mine. "Germany was driven to them long ago; France, Italy, Austria, Holland, Belgium, and, finally, we English, all had to follow. And you, in the States, you cannot continue to ignore the demand. It becomes more and more pressing all the time, you know, and the radicals take advantage of every denial of it."

Of course they do. The radicals are themselves evidences of the growing *consciousness* of a common, as well as an individual, problem of civilized living; and, as between the leadership that denies and that which acknowledges it, the majority of men (with the suffrage, now, remember) are bound either to sink into animal contentment or to follow radicals, like the Socialists, who not only recognize, but rejoice in, the work to be done; and, burning with their faith, offer not only hope, but something for every man to do; and not only a way out, but—a heaven on earth. Absurd? Maybe it is, but don't I illustrate my own point? I'm looking for light, and I don't care where I get it. If I don't find it in one place, I'll try another; if the Republicans and the Democrats shed only gloom, I'll apply to the Socialists; if my old leaders say there is no light—why, then, I'll have to ask Debs.

Yes, Eugene V. Debs is the keeper of the Socialist heaven. Locomotive fireman; labor agitator; strike leader; he was jailed once, and the Socialists, who take advantage of the misery of men to win them over, converted Debs in his cell at Woodstock. And now he is the leader of the Socialist party. I must confess that I didn't want to take my Socialism from Debs. Having use only for the truth, not the excesses and fallacies, of Socialism, I desired to get the best possible view of it, so I had picked out another man to interview, a hard-headed, intellectual student. But if the Socialists preferred Debs, the "undesirable citizen," "the incendiary," who wrote: "Rouse ye, Slaves," and called for a mob to follow him to Idaho, why, I felt that in a sense it was their party, not mine. And so, when they nominated him (the third time) for president of the United States, I saw Debs.

I don't know how to give you my impression of this man; I suppose I can't; I can hardly credit it myself, and I wouldn't, I guess, if I hadn't discovered so often before that the world (in the French phrase, "all the world") hates a lover of the world. And that's what 'Gene Debs is: the kindest, foolishest, most courageous lover of man in the world. Nor am I the only one that thinks so. Horace Traubel says: "Debs has ten hopes to your one hope. He has ten loves to your one love. You think he is a preacher of hate. He is only a preacher of men. When Debs speaks a harsh word it is wet with tears." . . .

I met Debs at a Milwaukee Socialist picnic (25,000 paid admissions) where he was to speak, and, as he came toward me with his two hands out, I felt, through all my prejudice, that those hands held as warm a heart as ever beat. Warm for me, you understand, a stranger; and not alone for me; those two warm hands went out to all in the same way: the workers, their wives, their children; especially the children, who spring at sight right into Debs's arms. It's wonderful, really. And when, piloted, plucked at, through the jammed mass of waiting humanity, he went upon the platform to speak, he held out his handfuls of affection to the crowd. He scolded them. "Men are beginning to have minds," he said; "some of you don't know it." There was nothing demagogic about that speech. It was impassioned, but orderly; radical, but (granting the premises) logically reasoned. It was an analysis of the platforms and performances of the two old parties to show that they would do for Business as much as they dared and for Labor as little; and the conclusion was an appeal to the workers—not to vote for Debs; "I don't ask that," he said, and sincerely, too. "All I ask is that you think, organize, and go into politics for yourselves."

Delivered from a crouching attitude, with reaching hands and the sweat dripping from head and face, the speech fairly flew, smooth, correct, and truly eloquent. Debs is an orator. "If Debs were a priest," wrote Eugene Field, "the world would listen to his eloquence, and that gentle, musical voice and sad, sweet smile of his would soften the hardest heart."

Half the world does listen to Debs, and his eloquence does soften its heart. But it wasn't art that kept that Milwaukee crowd steaming out there in the sun and, at the close, drew it crushing down upon the orator. And it wasn't what he said, either; too much of the gratitude was expressed in foreign tongues. It was the feeling he conveys that he feels for his fellow men; as he does, desperately.

Debs is dangerous; it is instinct that makes one half of the world hate him; but don't. He loves mankind too much to be hurt of men; and that's the power in him; and that's the danger. The trouble with Debs is that he puts the happiness of the race above everything else: business, prosperity, property. Remarking this to him, I said lightly that he was, therefore, unfit to be president.

"Yes," he answered seriously, "I am not fitted either by temperament or by taste for the office, and if there were any chance of my election I wouldn't run. The party wouldn't let me. We Socialists don't consider individuals, you know; only the good of all. But we aren't playing to win; not yet. We want a majority of Socialists, not of votes. There would be no use getting into power with a people that did not understand; with a lot of office-holders undisciplined by service in the party; unpurged, by personal sacrifice, of the selfish spirit of the present system. We shall be a minority party first, and the cooperative commonwealth can come only when the people know enough to want to work together, and when, by working together to win, they have developed a common sense of common service, and a drilled-in capacity for mutual living and cooperative labor. I am running for president to serve a very humble purpose: to teach social consciousness and to ask men to sacrifice the present for the future, to 'throw away their votes' to mark the rising tide of protest and build up a party that will represent them. When Socialism is on the verge of success, the party will nominate an able executive and a clear-headed administrator; not—not Debs."

It may be deemed expedient to hang Debs some day, and that wouldn't be so bad; but don't try to hurt him. In the first place, it's no use. Nature has provided for him, as she provides for other sensitive things, a guard; she has surrounded Debs with a circle of friends who go everywhere with him, shielding, caring for, adoring him. They sat all through my interview, ready to accept what I might reject. So he gets back the affection he gives, and no strange hate can hurt him. It can hurt only the haters. And as for the hanging, he half expects that.

"How could you," I asked, "thinking as you do that Socialists must learn by party service and personal sacrifice to deserve power, how could you have put out that call for a mob to rescue Moyer, Haywood, and Pettibone?"

"Oh, that," he answered. "The 'Rouse ye, Slaves'? Why, my God, man, that was only a cry. That was pain. You know Colorado—"

Yes, I know Colorado. I know that there was, that there is now, and that it is planned that there shall be, no justice in that state; know it, too, from the unjust themselves. "But," I urged, "the folly of mob force."

"True," said Debs, hanging his head. "It was folly, but," he added, looking up as if frightened, "do you know, I sometimes think I am destined to do some wild and foolish, useless thing like that and—so go."

Debs has written much about John Brown. Socialists see the repetitions of history, they read it in parallels, and they have found in it heroes of their own. Debs's hero is John Brown.

"The most picturesque character, the bravest man, the most self-sacrificing soul in American history was hanged at Charlestown, Virginia, December 2, 1859." Thus Debs begins an article which fairly worships John Brown's "moral courage and single-hearted devotion to an ideal for all men and for all ages. He resolved," says Debs, "to lay his life on Freedom's altar and to face the world alone. How perfectly sublime!"

That's Debs, I suspect. His adoration of John Brown is a view into himself. It gives us the ideal and the dread; the use and the danger; the strength and the weakness of the man. One must allow for personality in an interview, and in this case we should not forget for one moment that we are dealing with a man who speaks and acts from his heart, not his head; who honestly believes that there is something wrong in the world—some one big, removable "it," which meanwhile works terrible injustice to his kind of people, and who, therefore, feels that he may do "some wild and foolish, useless thing like"—John Brown.

I had a foil for Debs, however. The interview proper was at the house of Victor L. Berger, "the bear," leader of the Wisconsin Socialist party, which has forceful minorities in the state legislature and the Milwaukee city council. Berger is the man that made a Socialist of Debs, and the teacher, a most aggressive personality, took a most aggressive part in his pupil's interview, which was fortunate. For Socialism seems to be a science. It is an interpretation of history; a theory of the evolution of society; no mere, man-dreamed Utopia, as I have thought, but a faith, a calculation that, since the economic forces which have brought man from savagery up to the present state of civilization are continuous, we can foresee the next inevitable step. But it takes no little study of economics and much reading in the mass of Socialist literature to speak with authority on the subject, and Berger—with a library coveted by the University of Wisconsin—is an acknowledged authority.

"We believe," said Debs (for example), "that Socialism would come without the Socialists."

"Ach," said Berger, with his strong German roll, "we know it. Can't we see it?"

"Yes," said Debs. "The trusts are wiping out the competitive system. They are a stage in the process of evolution: the individual; the firm; the corporation; the trust; and so, finally, the commonwealth. By killing competition and training men to work together, trusts are preparing for the cooperative stage of industry: Socialism."

"Then you would keep the trusts we have and welcome others?" I asked.

"Of course," he answered, and Berger nodded approval.

"They do harm now," I suggested.

"Yes," said Debs, but Berger boomed: "No; not the trusts. Private owners of the trusts do harm, yes; but not the trusts."

"Well, but how would you deal with the harm?"

"Remove 'em," snapped Berger, and Debs explained: "We would have the government take the trusts and remove the men who own or control them: the Morgans and Rockefellers, who exploit; and the stockholders who draw unearned dividends from them."

"Would you pay for or just take them?"

Berger seemed to have anticipated this question. He was on his feet, and he uttered a warning for Debs—in vain.

"Take them," Debs answered.

"No," cried Berger, and, running around to Debs, he stood menacingly over him. "No, you wouldn't," he declared. "Not if I was there. And you shall not say it for the party. It is my party as much as it is your party, and I answer that we would offer to pay."

It was a tense but an illuminating moment. The difference is typical and temperamental; and not only as between these two opposite individualities, but among Socialists generally. Debs, the revolutionist, argued gently that, since the system under which private monopolies had grown up was unjust, there should be no compromise with it. Berger, the evolutionist, replied angrily that it was not alone a matter of justice, but of "tactic"; and that tactics were settled by authority of the party.

"We (Socialists) are the inheritors of a civilization," he proclaimed, "and all that is good in it—art, music, institutions, buildings, public works, character, the sense of right and wrong—not one of these shall be lost. And violence, like that, would lose us much." Berger cited the Civil War: "All men can see now that it was coming years before 1861. Some tried to avert it then by proposing to pay for the slaves. The fanatics on both sides refused. We all know the result: slavery was abolished. But how? Instead of a peaceful evolution and an outlay of, say, a billion, it was abolished by a war which cost us nearly ten billion dollars and a million lives. We ought to learn from history, so I say we will offer compensation; because it seems just to present-day thought and will prove the easiest, cheapest way in the end. And anyhow," he concluded, "and besites, the party, it has decited that we shall offer to pay."

And Berger was orthodox. Looking up the point afterward, I found that the "authorities" are on his side; the party will offer compensation for property taken by eminent domain.

"Debs?" said Berger. "Debs, with the soft heart—Debs is the orator." And he meant "only" an orator. Berger loves his pupil's "soft heart," but he loves Socialism more, and so during the interview, while Debs was trying to convert me, "the bear" was intent upon the orthodoxy of my report; and while Debs's other friends sat close up around him, under the light of the lamp, to protect the man, Berger hovered about in the shadow, anxious, on guard, to protect—"the cause."

"To begin with," said Debs, without waiting for questions, "we Socialists know what the matter is: it's capitalism; and we know what the cure is: it's Socialism."

"Words," I muttered.

"No," said he, drawing near and reaching out his hands. "Capitalism is a thing, a system; it's the organization of society under which we all live. And it's wrong, fundamentally wrong. It is a system of competition for wealth, for the necessities of human life, and, a survival of the old struggle of the jungle, it forces the individual to be selfish, and rewards him for beating and abusing his fellow man. Profit is made the aim of all human effort, not use, not service. The competitive system sets man against man, class against class; it puts a premium upon hate; and love—the love of a man for his neighbor—is abnormal and all but impossible. The system crucifies the prophets and servants of mankind. It pays greed the most, honors highest the ruthless, and advances swiftest the unscrupulous. These are the fit to survive."

Debs seized my arm. "It's wrong, isn't it? It's inherently unjust, inhuman, unintelligent, and—it cannot last. The particular evils you write about, graft and corruption, and the others about which I speak, the poverty, crime, and cruelty, they are evidences of its weakness and failure; the signs that it is breaking down."

"Why not wait, then, for it to break down?"

Debs drew back, rebuffed. "Because we have minds," he said. "Man can understand, and he can ride, the economic forces which now toss him so helplessly about, as well as he can the sea. And, having intelligence, he should. For human intelligence also is a force of nature. It could assist the process of evolution by searching diligently for the root of all evils as they arise."

"Panics and graft?" I suggested. "War, child-labor, crime, poverty?"

"All," he declared, "all are traceable to one cause. Take the panic, for example. Men lie about it, cover it up. Why not look it in the face? It's the proof that capitalists cannot handle industry, business, no, nor even money. And how can they when they are thinking, not of perfecting the machinery of life, but only of making profits out of it! So they don't understand the panic. We Socialists do. The capitalists attribute it to a variety of causes, all but the right one: capitalism, profits.

"No, wait," said Debs, waving me back. "They produce more than they want themselves, don't they? Of course. They make goods to sell;

not for use, primarily, but to make a profit. That's their god; and that's the devil, really. For see:

"Reduce our eighty millions to one hundred and our great continent to an island. The hundred all are workers at first. Each produces all that he wants. That's a low order of society. By and by they improve the tools, specialize their labor, and produce more. Steam, for example, applied to big, invented tools, does the work of a hundred small tools. Each man multiplies his productive capacity a thousand times. Should not the hundred on the island have all that they need?"

"Unless the population has increased."

"The more men, the more they produce. Every worker that can get at a machine can produce more than he needs himself. No, the hundred and the children of the hundred should have all that they want. But they don't. And one reason is that some have much more than they need: in profits; capital; new capital, upon which, you understand, labor must earn interest and a profit, for profits come first under capitalism, and necessarily, or capital vanishes. But let's go on.

"Ten of the hundred own all the big new machines; twenty struggle along with the little old tools; and seventy have no tools at all of their own. The biggest, best tools are the trusts, and the ten who have them are the trust magnates, full-fledged capitalists. The twenty are beaten, but they don't understand that yet; they are crying out against the trusts just as labor used to mob machinery. Bryan represents them; he wants to return to the competitive system with its anarchy, waste, and wars. Taft represents the trust magnates, opposing only their necessary crimes. We Socialists represent the seventy, who are the bulk of the population and the key to the situation. Consumers, as well as producers, they are the market, and when 'too much' is produced they must buy the surplus. But they can't. Having no tools of their own, and prevented from organizing effectively, they compete for the chance to get at the tools and sell their labor. That puts wages down. Receiving only a pittance of what they produce, they can buy back only a pittance. The surplus grows, a load on the market, till the crash comes, production halts, men are discharged, prices fall, and—there's your panic."

"And the need of foreign markets," I suggested. "Why wouldn't the other islands meet the need?"

"They would, temporarily," said Debs. "If there were enough islands, capitalism and wage-slavery might go on forever. But there aren't enough and—the other islands have the same system."

"And the same panics," Berger grunted, "thank God."

Debs winced, and I, thinking (also, I guess) of the misery, exclaimed: "Why thank God?"

Debs answered: "Berger sees there the chance for a higher civilization."

"Where?" I asked.

WHAT CAUSES PANICS?

"Oh, don't you see?" Debs pleaded. "The limitations of the
world's market and the panics will force us some day to unite and
solve our problem. And what is it? It's the problem of distribution.
That of production is in the way of solution already. With machinery
constantly increasing the productive power of the worker, and the
trusts cutting out the waste and disorder of duplicated plants, man
can produce enough. The capitalists themselves say so when they
ascribe their panic to 'overproduction.' They are wrong there, of
course. The panic is due, not to overproduction, but to undercon-
sumption. No, the supply is there and so is the demand. The masses
haven't all they need, and yet there's an abundance, a surplus. The
hitch is in distribution. The capitalist, producing, not to supply the
demand, but to get his profit, seeks to make the Hindu buy shoes he
doesn't want, while the American at home goes about ill-shod because, don't you see, his wages, fixed by competition, won't enable
him and his kind to buy all they need. Profits, not losses, make panics;
and panics make losses. The losses drive more small capitalists into
the trusts or back to labor, and the suffering of all opens people's eyes,
spreads discontent, and stimulates action. Panics compel progress."

"And panics," said Berger, from somewhere in the dark, "panics are
periodic."

"Business men are becoming more intelligent," I observed. "They
are forming associations, combines, pools, and, as you've said, trusts.
They may govern production and distribution, too."

"They can't govern themselves," said Berger. "They can't control
prices, because they can't control their own human nature, which,
bred under the sordid profit system, gets too strong for them. If they
had one absolute trust, they might limit the output, but—"

THE PROBLEM OF DISTRIBUTION

"But why," cried Debs, seizing my coat sleeve, "why limit production while men are in need?"

"Well, then, they can raise wages."

"Ah," said Debs, "that would postpone the panic, and the crisis,
for a while, if it were feasible. But it isn't feasible. In the first place,

no one employer can raise wages. He must act with his competitors, and the meanest sets the pace. Thats why organized labor must raise its own wages. Capital can't do it.

"And there, by the way, you have the cause of child-labor. Many a well-meaning manufacturer would like to spare the children, but he can't. If one glass manufacturer employs boys and girls, the others must do the same. No, capitalists, too, are victims of the competitive system."

"But a trust?"

"A monopoly," Debs answered, "has potential competition to look out for. If it were too generous with wages, new competitors would seize the chance, by paying a living wage, to undersell the trust and buy it out. The system is ruthless, you see. The conflict between wages and profits is absolutely unavoidable. Capital and labor cannot get together for long. For assume now that there is one universal trust, privately run for profit, and no possibility of competition; even then capital couldn't raise wages high enough to make possible complete consumption of the surplus, without wiping out what capital calls 'legitimate profits.' And the moment capital does that, it abdicates."

"How would Socialism do it?"

"By abolishing profits," said Debs. "Socialism will be an entirely different system. It will produce for use, not profit; and production for use is practically unlimited. Socialist society could produce ten times as much as we do now, because a cultured civilization would have ten times as many wants as we have. But if we found we were making more of one kind of goods than people could use, we would decrease the attractiveness of labor in that branch and increase it in another; and with workers schooled as we would school them (and as Germany is training them now) labor would go much more easily from one machine to another."

"You think that is possible?"

"Why," said Debs, "we've just seen that capitalism does it in its brutal way. It drives men from one place to another by the blind force of panics and starvation. Under Socialism, all industry would be intelligently managed as a trust manages it now on a small scale. And, freed from the brutalizing temptation of profits, it would apply civilized remedies in a civilized spirit."

THE ROOT OF THE EVIL

"Then it's profits you want to abolish."

"That's it," said Debs. "We want the producers to get all they produce."

"Who are producers?"

"All who labor in any productive way, mentally or physically. We would get rid only of the capitalists, stockholders, and financiers, who rake off fortunes for themselves and leave property in machinery and wage-slaves to keep their children in idleness, folly, or vice, a curse to themselves and a burden on the race for ever and ever and ever."

"Who would stand the losses?"

"Those who stand them finally now, the masses. For capitalists may rise and capitalists may fail, but capital grows on forever."

"But if you took away the chance of profits, wouldn't you take away all incentive—"

Berger sprang up, groaning, and just as Debs answered "No," the bear said: "Yes." We looked at Berger. "Yes, I say," he thundered. "We take away all incentive to steal and graft and finance and over-produce and shut up the shop sudden. But," and he came around and stood over me, "you," he said, "you wouldn't write except to get paid? And you wouldn't come her and talk with us, except for profit? I get wages, good wages, but no more. Won't I run my paper except for profit, and help in politics except for graft? Bah! I love my work."

AS TO INCENTIVES

"Berger's right," said Debs. "We all would do our work, as most of us do it now, without the incentive of a fortune in prospect. Wage-workers haven't that. John Wanamaker, with all his millions, was proud to accept a job at $8,000 to run the Post Office. Jefferson didn't write the Declaration of Independence for pay. Wouldn't a fireman save a child's life if he didn't get sixty dollars a month? And Harriman —wouldn't he operate railroads for a salary? Of course he would."

"But," said Berger, "he wouldn't finance 'em except for the incentive of millions of profit."

"Ah, no," said Debs, pleading, "men are better than you think; they are nobler now, and less selfish than your 'economic man.' We have heroes of altruism under the present system."

"True," I said, "but we haven't enough of them to build a society on. Self-interest is safer than altruism."

"Socialists don't propose to substitute altruism for self-interest."

"But you'd level men down and destroy individuality."

"Haven't I got individuality," called Berger, "and Debs?"

"Yes," I laughed, "too much, and so have most Socialists; but you all are products of the capitalist system."

"But the capitalist system," Berger retorted, "doesn't it level most men down now? Yes, it takes all the individuality, all the courage,

self-respect, liberty, and beauty out of the great mass of men to produce a few—"

"And look at those few," said Debs. "I'll leave your civilization to
that test alone, the test of its most successful men: Harriman, Rockefeller, Morgan. They are the flowers of the system; not the roots, remember. No, the monstrous specimens we produce today of individual
greed, cruelty, selfishness, arrogance, and—charity; not love, and not
justice, but degrading, corrupting, organized charity—these are one of
the results of the struggle for life and riches, and the other is that
beast—the mob."

Debs paused; then, more quietly: "There would be emulation after
competition is abolished. Men would vie in skill and service, and that
would produce individuality and character, though of a different sort.
A society where all men were safe would produce more such real men
and women as you find in the well-to-do class now. We would level
up, not down. We would let human nature develop naturally. And—
this you must believe—if we took away the fear of starvation on the
one hand and on the other the tremendous rewards for crookedness
and exploitation; removed all incentives to base self-seeking, and ar-
ranged things so that the good of the individual ran, not counter to,
as at present, but parallel with, the good of society, why, then, at last,
human nature would stand erect, manlike, frank, free, affectionate,
and happy."

"But we are off on the cure," I said. "Let's get back to what the
matter is."

"It's this," said Debs. "Some men live off other men."

"But how does that account for war, for example, and graft; political
corruption, ignorance, child-labor, crime, and poverty?"

WAGE-SLAVES

"We've accounted for poverty," said Debs. "We see the mass of
men working for the few. That's what we call wage-slavery, and it is
slavery. You say they might quit work; that the boss will let them
go. But I tell you the fear of starvation is the boss's slave driver. They
don't dare quit. You can't leave a trust and get back, and maybe the
trust controls the work in your trade. And then there's the blacklist.
Well, the wage-slaves work in competition, and they produce goods
that they need but haven't enough money to buy. That's poverty. And
the measure thereof is the riches of the exploiters of labor, industry,
and finance, and of their children till vice exhausts the family and re-
turns the grafted wealth through the dives and divorce courts back

to society. And there's one cause of capitalistic vice accounted for, as well as of poverty. And the other cause of poverty is the waste of competition and the artificial halt of production to keep up prices and profits."

"And crime?"

"Petty and professional crime," said Debs, "are a result of poverty; high crime springs from wealth-seeking."

"But vice, intemperance?"

"Frances Willard began her career telling working people that they wouldn't be so poor if they weren't so intemperate. She closed saying that the poor weren't poor because they drank; they drank because they were poor."

"But the rich drink," I protested.

"Idly," said Debs. "What else have they to do? Among busy businessmen, intemperance is rare, and when it occurs is inherited or due to the abnormal tension of the gamble which much business is now; an abnormal vice itself.

THE CRUELTY OF CAPITALISM

"Child-labor we have touched on before," Debs continued. "It is simply the meanest form of the exploitation of human beings by human beings, and, as I showed, is due, not to any inherent cruelty in the employer, but to the system of which he also is a victim—the capitalistic system which puts profits first and children—"

"How does your theory account for political corruption?" I asked.

"Why," said Debs, "you know about that. That's the capitalist class corrupting government to maintain them and their system of labor exploitation."

"I don't know that at all," I objected. "Not all businessmen take part in the corruption of politics. Only those do that have privileges from the government, franchises, and the like."

"Oh," said Debs, "you are thinking only of the big businesses, the railroads, public utilities, and so forth, which attend to the corruption of politics directly. But they do it for the rest of their class."

"No, they don't," I contradicted. "They do it for themselves. They don't know they belong to a class."

"I don't charge all of them with class consciousness," Debs answered. "Some of them do understand, but, whether they are intelligent or not, in that way they do make the government represent the business class. And, as for the smaller businessmen, they get the benefit. They contribute to campaign funds, and that's the big source of corruption, or, at any rate, they vote for one or the other of the two parties which the big fellows have corrupted and control, both of them."

"For privileges," I insisted. "Why isn't that the root of the evil?"

Debs shook his head, and, taking my arm in both hands, he said: "No, it's deeper than that. It's profits. The big fellows corrupt and rob railroads, insurance companies, banks; they finance and exploit the corporations and trusts. What governmental privilege is there in these businesses to explain the corruption of them?"

I'll have to let the Single-Taxers answer that. I can't. It's crucial, but I was stumped, and Debs went on:

"Privilege won't account for it all. Profit, gain, private property, in land and natural resources, machinery, and all means of production, that is at the bottom of it. And if you call these privileges, why, very well, I'll go along with you. For I believe myself that wage-slavery, the power to exploit labor and live off one's fellow men, is a privilege; the greatest privilege left since chattel slavery."

"How do profits account for war?" I said.

"We saw the cause of wars," he answered, "when we looked around for foreign markets."

"And bad workmanship," I proceeded, "one of the worst evils of the day?"

PROFITS AND BAD WORK

"We remarked," said Debs, "that captains of industry were turned from productive effort to finance. Capitalism will take a man who is a natural-born operator, say, of a railroad, make him president, and pay him salary enough to make him want more—profits. He gambles. He is taken into Wall Street; he sees how easy it is to exploit and finance. He is fascinated; he neglects operation; the railroad suffers; people are killed. Bad work that—for profits, for fascinating unearned profits.

"So with the worker," Debs added. "Do you teach him, by example and precept, to love to turn a piece of wood to fit a place? No. He doesn't know where the piece is to go. He works without interest, to live; he must; he works for wages. He sees the exploiters making their money easily; he hears industrial leaders, dishonest and self-indulgent themselves, insisting upon his honesty and industry. He understands; if he does more and better work his employer gets the benefit, not he. He rebels; he catches the capitalistic spirit. His boss robs him and the public; so he loafs, skimps, and robs the boss. All he is after is all the boss is after—money. That's the system."

"Now for your remedy: Socialism," I said. "What is it?"

WHAT IS SOCIALISM?

"You know the old stock definition," Debs answered. " 'The co-operative control and the democratic management of the means of production.' I'll try another: Socialism is the next natural stage in the evolution of human society; an organization of all men into an ordered, cooperative commonwealth in which they work together, consciously, for a common purpose: the good of all, not of the few, not of the majority, but of all."

"How would that induce the worker to do good work?"

"Well, if there were no inspiration in the idea of a common good there would be the assurance of a full return for the product of his labor."

"But how could such a complicated system give any such assurance?"

"By abolishing capitalists and all nonproducers."

"But managers—organizers?"

"They would be well paid. Men would be paid according to their social use; skill and ability would count, but so would the disagreeableness of a job; to get it done, society would have to make it attractive somehow—with short hours or big pay. For men would be free, you understand; much freer than now, and not only industrially, but politically, intellectually, religiously—every way. We would have no churches that didn't dare preach Christianity. But the point is that nobody would get such pay as Rockefeller gets now."

"Not even if he corrupted business and government and churches and colleges and men," said Berger.

"But Rockefeller did a service, you say yourselves," I retorted, "when he socialized the oil industry."

"Yes," said Debs, "but hasn't he been paid enough? A billion, they say. That's too much; but let him have it. All we Socialists say is that he should not be allowed to buy up railroads and mines and natural resources, and neither should oil consumers go on paying his children fortunes for generations. No, we must get rid of the Rockefellers, and keep only the organization they build up."

"But," I challenged, "If you took away Rockefeller's trust, wouldn't the other trust builders stop work?"

"Men don't organize trusts because they want to," said Debs, "but because they must. Competition drives them to it, that and their instinct for organization. Trust building can't be stopped; you might as well try to stop an ocean current."

WOULD MEN WORK UNDER SOCIALISM?

"But how would Socialism secure the services of eminent talent like that of the great organizers, instinctive operators, and natural managers?"

"The words you use to describe them, 'instinctive,' 'natural,' show that you think of them as born to a kind of work," said Debs. "They would want to do that kind of work. They couldn't help falling into it, and Socialism would offer such men greater incentives and more opportunities than they have now: pay according to service, public appreciation, and the chance they yearn for: to do good work unfretted (and uncorrupted) by grafting high financiers who are keen, not for excellence (look at our railroads), but for—profits. We would release the art instinct of the race."

"Geniuses might respond," I said, "but how about ordinary men?"

"All able-bodied persons of age would have to work," said Debs, "but they want to. I've heard convicts beg to be allowed to break stone. Man must be active, and a society that produced for use and not for profits would have plenty of work to have done, and all would have to help do it, excepting only the incapable. For them society must provide, as it does now, only better; more regularly, with justice, not charity. The first thing the Socialists abroad went after was the old-age pension, which gives worn-out workers the *right* to draw on society for sustenance. We want to remove from the earth the fear of starvation."

"How, then, will you deal with loafers and vicious persons?"

"They are abnormal," said Debs, "and, by removing the cause, poverty and riches, we should soon have no more of them. The idle children of the present rich would be without their graft, but they would foresee their predicament, and the best of them would go to work. Some of them seem to inherit from their parents talents which capitalistic society now gives them every incentive to neglect. Under Socialism—an inspiration, you realize, as well as an organization—they would probably exercise their abilities for the common good and their own greater satisfaction."

"Good," I said; "but the idle poor?"

"They are made what they are just as the idle rich are," said Debs. "Take a willing worker, overwork and underpay him, keep him on the verge, and then when he and his kind cannot consume what they produce, discharge him. He leaves his family to hunt a job, and, finding none, tramps or commits a crime. His children suffer, go young to work; they learn that their father is a bum or a crook. They are discouraged. The father drinks; they drink. Their children are, the best of them, perhaps, criminals, and the others, vagrants. This you see, and you ask me what Socialism will do with them? I'll tell you: we will treat, with physicians, as sick, the children that have inherited weak or wicked tendencies from parents and grandparents who lived under capitalism." Debs paused to restrain himself, then he concluded: "And we will stop making more by abolishing the cause— poverty and riches."

SOCIALISM AND ART

"If there is no rich, leisure class, what will become of art and culture and manners?"

"They will become common," said Berger, and Debs said: "All men will have some leisure. They will come strong and well paid from their work, ready to enjoy healthily all the good things of the earth. There will be no ignorance. Education will be free, not only in the money sense, but intellectually. The schools will teach liberty and the trades, justice and democracy and work, beauty, truth, and the glory of labor, efficient and honorable. The arts will thrive, as they always have thriven, in a free, cultivated democracy."

"Who will do the dirty work?"

"Machines," said Berger, "which clean my house now."

"Yes," said Debs; "only machines that increase profits are introduced now. Apparatus of great utility exists, but is suppressed by capital because human strength is cheaper, and improvements reduce profits. You doubt that? Ask the telephone and telegraph monopolies about the patents they own and don't use. But let me answer the question fully. There always will be some work less attractive than other kinds, and we should have to offer more pay or shorter hours to induce men to do it; men who want time to do unproductive things."

"If some men would get more pay than others," I asked, "why, then, couldn't they accumulate property?"

SOCIALISM FOR PRIVATE PROPERTY

"They could," he answered. "Socialism does not abolish private property, except in the means of production. We want all men to have all they produce, all; *we* are for private property; it is capitalism that is against it. Under capitalism only the few can have property. And so with the home; and love. Capitalism is against homes. It makes it inexpedient for young workers to marry; that makes for prostitution, which is against the home. And so is the tenement system of housing, which is good for profits and rents, but bad for homes and—love. And so is marriage for money against love."

"But, Debs, you must admit that you Socialists preach class war, and that engenders hate."

"No, no," he answered, rising all his great height over me, "we do not preach hate; we preach love. We do not teach classes; we are opposed to classes. That is capitalism again. There are classes now, and we say so. Why not? It's true, terribly true. But it's exactly that we are trying to beat. The struggle of the best men now is to rise from the working into the exploiting class. We teach the worker not to strive to rise out of his class; not to want to be an employer, but to stay with his fellow workers, and by striving all together, industrially, financially, politically, learn to cooperate for the common good of the working class to the end that some day we may abolish classes and have only workers—all kinds of workers, but all producers. Then we should have no class at all, should we? Only men and women and children."

"How are you Socialists going to get all this?"

"We Socialists aren't going to get it," said Debs. "It's coming out of the natural evolution of society, and the trusts are doing more toward it than we. Socialists are only preparing the minds of men for it, like the labor unions. They are taking the egotism out of men; subordinating the good of the individual to that of the union; and teaching self-sacrifice and service.

"So with us. The party is the thing. It is governed by its members, who must pay to belong to it, and all perform services besides. They work, write, speak—what they can. But it's theirs, our party is. They elect officers and delegates; they nominate tickets; and they are taught to vote a straight party vote, no matter how hopeless the contest. That's often a sacrifice of the present for the future, of the individual for society. But isn't that good? That's discipline. It's an education in cooperation. Their reward will come when, by and by, we shall have everywhere, as we have here in Wisconsin now, a minority in office of representatives trained in that school, enlightened as to general economic and moral principles, and inspired with an ideal that is as fine as any religion in the world ever had—the good of all."

"That's slow," I said, "and you, Debs, are impatient."

FOUNDATION LOVE OF MAN FOR MAN

"Yes," he said, "I am in a hurry, but Socialism isn't. Socialism is the most patient of reforms, but also it is the surest, and the truest. For we believe in man and in the possibility of the love of man for man. We know that economic conditions determine man's conduct toward man, and that so long as he must fight him for a job or a fortune, he cannot love his neighbor. Christianity is impossible under capitalism. Under Socialism it will be natural. For a human being loves love and he loves to love. It is hate that is unnatural. Love is implanted deep in our hearts, and when things are rearranged so that I can help my fellow man best by helping myself, by developing all my skill and strength and character to the full, why, then, I shall love him more than ever; and if we compete it will be as artists do, and all good men, in skill, productiveness, and good works."

Theodore Roosevelt:
Debs as an Inciter to Murder

In May, 1911, the McNamara brothers were arrested for dynamiting the building of the San Francisco Examiner *in the midst of a heated labor dispute. They denied the charges, and a massive campaign for their defense was initiated by San Francisco labor leaders and Socialists. A few months later the brothers admitted their guilt, and the nation rocked from the implications of the new labor violence.*

Theodore Roosevelt, who liked to refer to a "progressive" as a "conservative who resolutely sets his face towards the future," lashed out at those among the radicals who continued to identify the McNamaras as legitimate parts of the labor movement. To Roosevelt, Debs and other radicals were only apologists for murderers. The article reflects TR's well known animosity toward radicals and his ever-present fear that class-based radicalism had not been eliminated in the new America.[1]

MURDER IS MURDER

Since the startling outcome of the McNamara trial certain apologists of these men have made themselves conspicuous by asserting that these depraved criminals, who have on their seared souls the murder of so many innocent persons—*all of them laboring people, by the way*—are "victims," or at worst "fanatics," who should receive sympathy because they were acting in what they regarded as a "war" on behalf of their class! The plea is monstrous in its folly and its wickedness. It is precisely the kind of plea sometimes advanced on behalf of a crooked man of great wealth caught bribing a legislature—that he has to do it to protect his business. We are not here dealing with any of the kinds of offenses incidental to the sudden and sweeping changes brought about by modern industrial conditions into which capitalists or labor men are sometimes drawn without any very great conscious moral turpitude on their part. We are dealing with crimes as old as the lawgiving from Sinai, with crimes—murder and theft— that have been prohibited ever since the decalogue was formulated.

---

[1] From *The Outlook* (December 16, 1911), pp. 901–2.

The murders committed by men like the McNamaras, although nominally in the interest of organized labor, differ not one whit in moral culpability from those committed by the Black Hand, or by any band of mere cutthroats, and are fraught with an infinitely heavier menace to society. Yet, great though the menace is to the community, the menace to the cause of honest organized labor is still greater, and no duty is more imperatively laid on the leaders of labor than the duty of affirmatively freeing themselves and their followers from the taint of responsibility for such criminals and such crimes. The labor leaders who have succeeded in identifying them with the cause of labor in the eyes of the public have rendered an evil service to that cause. Mr. Debs and the extremists of his type among the so-called political Socialists—I say so-called because Debs and his followers of the Emma Goldman kind are not Socialists at all in any true sense of the word, but mere inciters to murder and preachers of applied anarchy—and the labor leaders affiliated with them, have always boasted of the part they played in the trial of Moyer and Haywood; and in this case they repeated their familiar tactics, and held mass-meetings, and scattered broadcast papers and addresses in which they furiously denounced the effort to bring wrong-doers to justice, and sought to arouse every evil class instinct against all who upheld the cause of law or sought to put a stop to assassination and murderous violence. It is worth noting that since McNamara confessed his guilt, Mr. Moyer, the head of what purports to be a labor organization, is reported in the press as commenting upon it, not by denouncing McNamara for having committed the murder, but by denouncing him for having confessed it! Such denunciation is significant.

Murder is murder, and the foolish sentimentalists or sinister wrong-doers who try to apologize for it as an "incident of labor warfare" are not only morally culpable but are enemies of the American people, and, above all, are enemies of American wage-workers. In honorable contrast to these men stand the various labor leaders who have never asked for more than a fair trial for the McNamaras, whose purpose has only been to get justice, and who now sternly demand that murder shall be punished when committed in the nominal interest of labor precisely as under any other circumstances. I believe with all my heart in the American workingman; I believe with all my heart in organized labor, for labor must be organized in order to protect and secure its rights; and therefore with all my strength I urge my fellow citizens, the American men and women who earn their livelihood as wage-workers, to see that their leaders stand for honesty and obedience to the law, and to set their faces like flint against any effort to identify the cause of organized labor, directly or indirectly, with any movement which in any shape or way benefits by the commission of crimes of lawless and murderous violence.

Max Eastman:
Greek Drama in Cleveland—
The Trial of Eugene Debs

In 1913, Max Eastman became editor of The Masses, *a socialist magazine published by artists and writers. After that journal was suppressed for opposing U.S. entrance into World War I, Eastman founded* The Liberator, *which he edited until 1922. As a major literary radical, Eastman covered the trial of Debs for violation of the Espionage and Sedition Act in September 1918.*

Debs himself in young manhood had conceived and organized an industrial union, the American Railway Union, and conducted two of the most militant strikes in labor's history. That perhaps was his most signal achievement; in that direction lay his proper career. But he was caught away by the socialist idea in its milder and more wholesale aspect, the idea of reconstructing all society at a stroke by educating the voters and bringing the lower classes to the topmost seats of power. His chief gift, aside from loving kindness, in which he was a genius of the purest order, was for oratory. And it is not unnatural that upon seeing the light of Marxism as reflected in America in the early nineties, he should have turned to a wider audience and a more homiletical mode of attack. He remained a working-class rebel, however. He never got wound up in the intricate tangle of small threads of insincerity engendered by a career in temporary politics on a platform of ultimate revolution. Even while heading the party and conducting five campaigns as its candidate for president, he was still at heart a militant agitator—more accurately perhaps, a purehearted evangelist, an orator of the clear issue and the uncompromising ideal.

As a result he was singled out inevitably as the arch-traitor when the United States declared war on Germany in 1917, and the Socialists continued to denounce the war. He was arrested, indicted under the Espionage Act, and tried in the United States Court, essentially

---

[1] From "Greek Drama in Cleveland—The Trial of Eugene Debs," in Max Eastman, *Heroes I Have Known, Twelve Who Lived Great Lives* (New York: Simon and Schuster, 1942), pp. 46–48, 50–52, 55–61, 64–68. Reprinted by permission of Mrs. Max Eastman.

for treason to his country. This placed before him a choice: Whether to dodge and argue and hire lawyers to prove what was, of course, the fact, that he was not a traitor and had not even broken a law; or to ignore these niceties of superficial fact, and confront the state, as Socrates did, on terms of the underlying truth that their aims were unalterably opposed. . . .

He was tried in Cleveland, Ohio, in a courthouse across whose face is inscribed in gigantic stone letters the insolent sophism: "Obedience to Law Is Liberty." It was my good fortune to attend the trial, and witness a drama as clean-lined and fulfilling, as elevated above the ruck of ignoble and unconsecrated shop-and-market living, as anything in our history.

When I slipped into the crowded courtroom a pretty young man in a neat suit and a bow tie, a witness for the prosecution, was reading to the jury an antiwar speech that Debs had made in the neighboring city of Canton. The young man was embarrassed to find so much wit and eloquence in his mouth. . . . He was a stenographer who had been hired by the Socialist party itself to take down Debs's speech. He was concerned now to make it evident that he was patriotic and favored the prosecution. He would try to express indignation by looking up with compressed lips at the jury after what he thought must be a particularly traitorous passage in Debs's speech. But the passage would not turn out very traitorous, nor he very indignant. He wore little lobes of hair in front of his ears—and perfume, I think, on his handkerchief—and the wealth of Debs's personality shone through him as he read, so that he became in the eyes of the onlookers very small.

Another report of the speech had been taken by an agent of the Department of Justice, but he had been too warmly interested to write down more than half of it. . . . Two or three newspaper reporters, now clad in khaki, were also introduced to corroborate the general impression that Debs had made a speech at Canton, and that he had made it to a crowd. Estimates of the crowd varied from two hundred to fifteen hundred. At least, he had made it out loud, and from a bandstand not decorated with a flag, and just after a reading of the Declaration of Independence. These reporters were respectful of Debs and not very happy on the stand. . . .

Nothing mattered much in those cases but the indictment. After they had dragged a man into court in the high state of patriotic tension then prevailing, and a state official had announced to a jury in a resounding voice that the government believed this man guilty of inciting a mutiny in the United States Army, of stirring up disloyalty in his countrymen, of obstructing the enlistment of soldiers, of en-

couraging resistance to the United States of America, and promoting
the cause of the enemy—it was about all done but the verdict. . . .
The jury's . . . reaction to a prophet of proletarian revolt was as
simple to predict. They were about seventy-two years old, worth
fifty to sixty thousand dollars, retired from business, from pleasure,
and from responsibility for all troubles arising outside of their own
families. An investigator for the defense computed the average age
of the entire venire of one hundred men; it was seventy years. Their
average wealth was over fifty thousand dollars. In the twelve finally
chosen to sit in judgment upon Debs, every man save one, an aging
contractor, was a retired farmer or a retired merchant. . . . "There is
something pathetic," Debs remarked to me after they had judged him,
"about dressed-up faces—smug bodies. If they had been dressed in
rags it would have been all right."

And then he added something which reveals, as I look far back
upon it, his limitations as well as his charm.

"What a contrast to turn toward the back of the courtroom and
see a little group of beautiful Socialists with stars for eyes—you can
always tell them!"

Debs was the tenderest of strong men. He was a poet, and even more
gifted with poetry in private speech than in public oratory. Every
instant and incident of his life was deep and sacred to him. He handled
his body, and his mind too, all the time, as though each were an extremely delicate instrument. He was present with entire spirit and
concentration in every minutest motion that he had made. His tongue
would dwell upon a "the" or an "and" with a kind of earnest affection
for the humble that threw the whole accent of his sentences out of the
conventional mold, and made each one seem a special creation of the
moment. He was tall and long of finger like a New Hampshire farmer,
and yet just as vivid, intense, and exuberant with amiability as the
French. A French Yankee is what he was. And the motions of his
hands and body were as beautiful, and his spirit as beautiful, as anything I have seen in any man.

The religion of Socialism is compounded of the passions both of
fighting and of love. And Debs knew how to fight. . . . But that was
not his genius. His genius was for love—for the old real love, the
miracle love that utterly identifies itself with the needs and wishes
of others. For that reason it was like a sacrament to meet him, to have
that warm, rapierlike attention concentrated on you for a moment.
For that reason he was so much mightier than many who are more
astute and studious of the subtleties of politics and oratory. . . .

When the clumsy-thumbed prosecutor, with his round jowl and
long sharpened nose, got through laboring forth what he had in proof

that Debs said what he said, and grumbled, "We rest," there was a pause. Debs looked up at Stedman. Stedman looked over at the prosecutor.

"Let's see—you rest?" he said. "*We* rest!"

A kind of numb surprise possessed the court. Nothing was said for a while. The prosecutor was disappointed. He would be deprived of his sport of bulldozing witnesses for the defense. Well—he would make up for it by denouncing the defendant later on. Finally the judge declared a recess of ten minutes, and everybody with a good seat settled to wait.

"Mr. Debs will conduct his own defense," said Stedman when the court assembled again, and he went over to the press table and sat down. The other attorneys sat down. Then everybody waited and watched, intently, as though for lightning.

Debs got up very deliberately, gathering some papers, and he looked in the eyes of his judge a full minute while the room grew very still, before he began, courteously and quietly, but with that tense magnetic precision of his, to discuss the only question that seemed able to engage his fervent interest, the question whether what he had said in his speech at Canton was true. . . .

It was dark when Debs began speaking, though only two o'clock in the afternoon, and as he continued it grew steadily darker, the light of the chandeliers gradually prevailing, and the windows turning black as at nighttime with gathering thunderclouds. His utterance became more clear and piercing against the augmenting shadow, and it made the simplicity of his faith seem almost like a portent in that time of terrible and dim events. It was as though love and the very essence of light were inspired to lead the world straight on into the black heart of storm and destruction.

Debs had been accused of "sympathy for the Bolsheviki" in Russia. He declared his sense of solidarity with them, and his knowledge that they are wantonly lied about in our newspapers, as the few who want to better the world have always been lied about, as Christ was lied about—and Socrates—accused and persecuted. . . .

That was the manner of Debs's defense to the end. He did not offer any argument upon the evidence. He did not once employ his gift of ironic confutation, which might have exposed weak points in the case of the prosecution. He did not even condescend, as his attorneys urged, to present the outline of a legal argument upon which a juryman so disposed might rest the emotional wish to acquit him. With a very genial—and privately quite uproarious—scorn for the whole legal apparatus in which they were trying to tie up his clear-motivated intelligence, he stubbornly declined to come down from the region of truth and noble feeling where he lived. He compelled the jury to come up there and listen to him, or not listen at all.

They came up, and then after he had stopped talking they descended again, a little bewildered and uncomfortable, and carried out their business in the routine way. Assuming there was a single man of decent sensitivity among the twelve, the district attorney, Mr. Wertz, did all that lay in his power to lose the case with that man. It would not have been very difficult for anybody to convict Debs after his own speech—he made it so evident that he would not take it as a personal judgment and that it would not and could not enter into his soul in the slightest degree. He had not asked the jury not to convict him, but only, assuming that they would, had tried to make it clear in his own words what they were convicting him for. But after this ungainly, gross official with a high whine through his teeth had poured raw insults out of his mouth for an hour, so that everyone in the court, from the judge to the stiff little bailiff, was mortified, and his own more clever assistant squirmed in his chair with embarassment, it became really difficult even for the most patriotic citizen to do his duty. I credit the prosecuting attorney with five of the six hours that this jury had to stay out recovering from the emotional impact of the scene they had witnessed. . . .

"If this old yo wants to go to the penitentiary I've got no objection, . . . Congress has pledged the resources of the United States to win this war, and the resources of the United States are the body of Eugene Debs just as much as the cattle and the crops. . . . These doctrines lead to nothing but trouble and distraction. . . . They ought to be tried for treason, the whole outfit. If it had been any other country in the world but the United States, they'd have faced a firing squad long ago. Internationalism, he says. I'll tell you what internationalism is. Pitch all the nations into one pot with the Socialists on top, and you've got internationalism. . . ."

So it flowed out of his mouth for an hour. Then the judge adjourned the court until morning, and the jury tottered away, and we all walked over to the hotel with Debs, to find the humor in the situation, and hear its fine points enjoyed as only one looking down from a secure elevation could enjoy them.

The next . . . evening the jury, hardened up at last to their unwelcome task, tottered back to their seats. Cyrus R. Stoner, aged fifty-eight years, the youngest among them, rendered the verdict of guilty. Debs was released in custody of his attorneys, and the court adjourned for another day while the judge should take counsel with himself as to the appropriate length of the sentence.

On Saturday morning Stedman offered argument for a new trial on the ground that the prosecution had made much of the "St. Louis proclamation" of the Socialist party, which Debs had not mentioned in his speech at Canton. But Debs mentioned the St. Louis proclamation with some affection in his speech before the jury, and so the judge was justified in denying that there was ground here for a new trial.

The motion was overruled. The district attorney moved for the imposition of sentence, and the clerk asked: "Eugene V. Debs, have you anything further to say in your behalf before the Court passes sentence upon you?" Again Debs rose and walked slowly forward, again paused until the little clamorous routine of personal and particular event had dropped away:

"Your Honor, years ago I recognized my kinship with all living beings, and I made up my mind that I was not one bit better than the meanest of earth. I said then, I say now, that while there is a lower class, I am in it, while there is a criminal element, I am of it, while there is a soul in prison, I am not free. . . ."

Woodrow Wilson:
Debs—"Traitor to His Country."

Despite a massive and popular campaign on behalf of amnesty for the imprisoned Eugene V. Debs, President Woodrow Wilson refused to issue a presidential pardon, even after armistice had been declared.[1] It was left for the conservative Republican Warren G. Harding to issue an executive Christmas pardon for Debs on December 23, 1921.

One of the things to which [Woodrow Wilson] paid particular attention at this time was the matter of the pardon of Eugene V. Debs. The day that the recommendation for pardon arrived at the White House, he looked it over and examined it carefully, and said: "I will never consent to the pardon of this man. I know that in certain quarters of the country there is a popular demand for the pardon of Debs, but it shall never be accomplished with my consent. Were I to consent to it, I should never be able to look into the faces of the mothers of this country who sent their boys to the other side. While the flower of American youth was pouring out its blood to vindicate the cause of civilization, this man, Debs, stood behind the lines, sniping, attacking, and denouncing them. Before the war he had a perfect right to exercise his freedom of speech and to express his own opinion, but once the Congress of the United States declared war, silence on his part would have been the proper course to pursue. I know there will be a great deal of denunciation of me for refusing this pardon. They will say I am cold-blooded and indifferent, but it will make no impression on me. This man was a traitor to his country and he will never be pardoned during my administration."

[1] From Joseph P. Tumulty, *Woodrow Wilson as I Know Him* (New York: Doubleday, Page and Co., 1921), pp. 504–5.

Haywood Broun:
The Miracle of Debs

Haywood Broun, a founder of the American Newspaper Guild, was considered to be one of the most prominent prounion and liberal journalists of the late 1920s and early 1930s. Although he had never met Debs, Broun's estimate of the Socialist leader as a "sentimental Socialist" reflected the widespread compassion and sympathy that Debs as a person had been able to produce.[1] He was speaking only for himself, but Broun undoubtedly mirrored the way in which thousands of Americans thought of Eugene V. Debs.

Eugene V. Debs is dead and everybody says that he was a good man. He was no better and no worse when he served a sentence at Atlanta.

I imagine that now it would be difficult to find many to defend the jailing of Debs. But at the time of the trial he received little support outside the radical ranks.

The problem involved was not simple. I hated the thing they did to Debs even at the time, and I was not then a pacifist. Yet I realize that almost nobody means precisely what he says when he makes the declaration, "I'm in favor of free speech." . . .

It would have been better for America to have lost the war than to lose free speech. I think so, but I imagine it is a minority opinion. However, a majority right now can be drummed up to support the contention that it was wrong to put Debs in prison. That won't keep the country from sending some other Debs to jail in some other day when panic psychology prevails.

You see, there was another aspect to the Debs case, a point of view which really begs the question. It was foolish to send him to jail. His opposition to the war was not effective. A wise dictator . . . would have given Debs better treatment than he got from our democracy.

Eugene Debs was a beloved figure and a tragic one. All his life he led lost causes. He captured the intense loyalty of a small section of our people, but I think that he affected the general thought of his

---

[1] From Haywood Broun, *It Seems to Me, 1925–1935* (New York: Harcourt, Brace and Company, 1935), pp. 35–39. Reprinted by permission of Mrs. Constance Broun and Heywood Hale Broun.

time to a slight degree. Very few recognized him for what he was. It became the habit to speak of him as a man molded after the manner of Lenin or Trotzky. And that was a grotesque misconception. People were constantly overlooking the fact that Debs was a Hoosier, a native product in every strand of him. He was a sort of Whitcomb Riley turned politically minded.

It does not seem to me that he was a great man. At least he was not a great intellect. . . . Certainly he had character. There was more of goodness in him than bubbled up in any other American of his day. He had some humor, or otherwise a religion might have been built up about him, for he was thoroughly Messianic. And it was a strange quirk which set this gentle, sentimental Middle Westerner in the leadership of a party often fierce and militant.

Though not a Christian by any precise standard, Debs was the Christian-Socialist type. That, I'm afraid, is outmoded. He did feel that wrongs could be righted by touching the compassion of the world. Perhaps they can. It has not happened yet. Of cold, logical Marxianism, Debs possessed very little. He was never the brains of his party. I never met him, but I read many of his speeches, and most of them seemed to be second-rate utterances. But when his great moment came a miracle occurred. Debs made a speech to the judge and jury at Columbus after his conviction, and to me it seems one of the most beautiful and moving passages in the English language. He was for that one afternoon touched with inspiration. If anybody told me that tongues of fire danced upon his shoulder as he spoke, I would believe it. . . . The speech which Debs made is to me a thing miraculous, because in it he displayed a gift for singing prose which was never with him on any other day of his life. . . .

Something was in Debs, seemingly, that did not come out unless you saw him. I'm told that even those speeches of his which seemed to any reader indifferent stuff, took on vitality from his presence. A hard-bitten Socialist told me once, "Gene Debs is the only one who can get away with the sentimental flummery that's been tied onto Socialism in this country. Pretty nearly always it gives me a swift pain to go around to meetings and have people call me 'comrade.' That's a lot of bunk. But the funny part of it is that when Debs says 'comrade' it's all right. He means it. That old man with the burning eyes actually believes that there can be such a thing as the brotherhood of man. And that's not the funniest part of it. As long as he's around I believe it myself."

With the death of Debs, American Socialism is almost sure to grow more scientific, more bitter, possibly more effective. The party is not likely to forget that in Russia it was force which won the day, and not persuasion.

I've said that it did not seem to me that Debs was a great man in life, but he will come to greatness by and by. There are in him the seeds of symbolism. He was a sentimental Socialist, and that line has dwindled all over the world. Radicals talk now in terms of men and guns and power, and unless you get in at the beginning of the meeting and orient yourself, this could just as well be Security Leaguers or any other junkers in session.

The Debs idea will not die. To be sure, it was not his first at all. He carried on an older tradition. It will come to pass. There can be a brotherhood of man.

PART THREE

DEBS IN HISTORY

Arthur M. Schlesinger, Jr.: Debs, The Popular Socialist[1]

The history of American radicalism is to most Americans largely a forgotten and obscure history. It becomes a collection of vignettes—lonely men talking earnestly in small groups, passionate men pleading with curious and indifferent crowds, courageous men defeated by power or by apathy. When radicalism becomes respectable, when it acquires the apparatus which guarantees an ordered legacy for the historian, then it probably ceases to be truly radical. Eugene V. Debs was keenly aware of the corruption of respectability. He took his chance with history rather than with the historian.

His career was a career of dedication to unpopularity. He rejected success in the terms of his age—success as a respectable labor leader or as a complaisant politician; he declared war on his own age in the name, as he conceived it, of the next. Yet he carried on this fight in a spirit so authentically American—so recognizably in the American democratic tradition—that under his leadership the Socialist movement in this country reached its height. The result of this mixture of qualities—the robust Socialism, the indisputable Americanism, the dedication without compromise—has been to give Debs the somewhat shadowy role he now occupies on the periphery of our history. His friends achieved a sentimental hagiography about him which can strike a later generation only as naïve hero worship. His enemies, unable to exclude Debs from American history, took advantage of the broad and heart-warming Hoosier strain in him. They have sought to disarm Debs by turning him into a folksy character out of the American past.

Eugene Victor Debs was born in a plain wooden shack in Terre Haute, Indiana, on November 5, 1855. His parents, who had come to the United States from Alsace in 1849, were frugal, hard-working people. Of ten children, six—Eugene, his devoted brother Theodore, and

[1] From Introduction to *The Writings and Speeches of Eugene V. Debs*, (New York: The Hermitage Press, 1948), pp. v–xiii. Reprinted by permission of the author.

four sisters—reached adult age. The family group was an exceptionally happy one. It not only gave Debs the capacity for simple human tenderness, which played so large a role in his life, but awakened in him a wide-ranging intellectual curiosity. Victor Hugo was prominent in the family library; and *Les Misérables* had a marked impact on Debs's emotions as well as (less fortunately) on his rhetoric. . . .

It was the winter of 1894–95. The country was still low in depression. Economic collapse and unemployment had sharpened business-labor antagonisms. The Homestead strike of 1892 had seemed to reveal a vengeful determination on the part of the business community to stamp out independent labor organizations. Debs himself had accepted the weakness of craft unions in such a fight; but his hope had been that a giant industrial union might be able to fight a giant industry to a standstill. The Pullman strike now showed that he had not reckoned on the press, the courts, and the army. All the institutions of capitalistic society appeared to be in league against the workingman.

Yet, at the same time, mutterings of agrarian dissatisfaction were swelling to a roar in the name of Populism. Labor was showing new strength. A fresh literature of radicalism scoffed at palliatives and demanded basic social reconstruction. Debs, brooding in his cell at Woodstock, tried to make sense out of the Pullman débâcle. The more he thought, the clearer it became. "In the gleam of every bayonet and the flash of every rifle *the class struggle was revealed.*" The Pullman strike, he concluded, had been a "practical lesson in Socialism." He turned to *The Co-operative Commonwealth* of Lawrence Gronlund, an early American attempt to domesticate Marx; he recalled Edward Bellamy's *Looking Backward* and the writings of Robert Blatchford, the English Socialist; he found the works of Karl Kautsky "clear and conclusive." An eager Milwaukee Socialist named Victor L. Berger appeared at Woodstock one day, delivered Debs an impassioned lecture on Socialism, and presented him with a copy of Marx's *Capital.*

A tough and pragmatic trade unionist had entered the Woodstock jail. A radical well on the way to Socialism departed six months later. Something like one hundred thousand people jammed the streets of Chicago to greet him on his return. The tall, lean man, bald, beak-nosed, smooth-shaven, his face already beginning to be lined and wrinkled, harangued the crowd in bold, searching language.

Debs gathered together the battered remnants of the ARU behind Bryan in 1896, though he had no enthusiasm for the free silver panacea. In June 1897, he transformed the ARU into the Social Democratic party of the United States. "There is no hope for the toiling masses of my countrymen," he said, "except by the pathways mapped out by Socialists, the advocates of the cooperative commonwealth."

Even in 1897, however, there was little unanimity among Socialists as to which pathway was the right one—and great confidence that the next person's deviation was fatal. Daniel De Leon, the brilliant and doctrinaire leader of the Socialist Labor party, was intent on achieving dogmatic purity at the expense of almost everything else, including political effect. In 1900 the more practical-minded wing of the Socialist Labor party, headed by Morris Hillquit, long chafing under De Leon's tight reins, went over to the Social Democrats to create what became in 1901 the Socialist party. In 1900 Debs, as presidential candidate of the two groups, polled nearly 100,000 votes.

Under Debs's fighting leadership, American Socialism now entered its period of national popularity. Debs himself remained curiously apart from the top direction of the Socialist movement. He could rival neither Hillquit as an organizer nor De Leon as a theoretician; he neither dominated party conventions nor contributed important new doctrines. But he had achieved a passionate sense of the urgency of the class struggle and a passionate vision of a future society liberated from capitalism. "It is simply a question of capitalism or socialism, of despotism or democracy," he would say, "and those who are not wholly with us are against us." No other Socialist could communicate the vision and the urgency with the intensity of Debs. He became one of the great American orators.

He brought to the party a devotion, an evangelical energy, and, above all, a profoundly intuitive understanding of the American people. Men and women loved Debs even when they hated his doctrines. His sweetness of temper, his generosity and kindliness, his sensitivity to pain and suffering, his perfect sincerity, his warm, sad smile and his candid gray eyes, were irresistible. He was a complete Hoosier, in sentimentality as well as in practicality. "There are two words in our language forever sacred to memory," he could write, ". . . Mother and Home! Home, the heaven upon earth, and mother its presiding angel." Such specialists in midwestern sentimentalism as James Whitcomb Riley and Eugene Field loved him. . . .

As a campaigner, he was intense and tireless. In 1904 he started on September 1, crisscrossed the country and wound up in Terre Haute, speaking every day and often several times a day. His total vote shot up above 400,000. In 1908 the Socialist party hired the famous "Red Special" which toured the country, stopping at large towns and small, leaving behind vivid memories of a tall, gaunt, earnest man, leaning far over the edge of the back platform, underlining his statements with emphatic gestures of a long, bony forefinger, shouting hoarse-voiced indictments of a selfish and ruthless capitalism. His vote increased only about 20,000 over 1904. But Socialist confidence was not

diminished, and in 1912 Debs polled 900,000 votes—almost 6 percent
of the total (the equivalent of over 2,500,000 votes in the 1944 election).

In the meantime, Debs in 1905 had helped found the Industrial
Workers of the World—the realization of his ancient dream of one
big union. Through the years he had been unsparing in his denunciation of the American Federation of Labor, which seemed to have
found a comfortable niche in the status quo. "The old forms of trade
unionism," cried Debs, "no longer meets the demands of the working class. . . . It is now positively reactionary, and is maintained,
not in the interests of the workers who support it, but in the interests
of the capitalist class who exploit the workers." So long as the working class was parcelled out among thousands of separate unions,
united economic and political action would be impossible. The IWW
provided new hope.

Was not Socialism in the United States now on the verge of meaning something? By 1912 the Socialist party had 118,000 dues-paying
members, of whom over a thousand held public office—including 56
mayors, over 300 aldermen, some state legislators, and one Congress-
man. It had five English dailies and 262 English weeklies as well as a
large number of foreign-language journals. Socialists controlled the
IWW; and a Socialist running against Samuel Gompers for the presidency of the AF of L received one third of the vote.

Yet already symptoms of decline were visible. If the AF of L was
too conservative, the IWW was too recklessly revolutionary. Socialists
like Debs who believed in political action and in trade unions condemned the syndicalist susceptibilities of the IWW, with the consequent contempt for politics and for honest collective bargaining and
the rise of the cult of "direct action." At the same time, Woodrow
Wilson's New Freedom, coming on top of Theodore Roosevelt's
Progressivism, was doing much to win back independent liberals to
the two-party system. Then, in the years after 1914, the war in Europe
became the absorbing issue. By 1916 a vote for Wilson seemed to
many the surest vote for peace. Debs, now sixty-one and ailing, could
not face another campaign. Allan Benson, the Socialist candidate,
polled only slightly over 500,000 votes.

War drove a wedge through the party. The Socialist majority held
firm against "militarism"; but an influential minority, including much
of the party's intellectual leadership, walked out. Debs was no pacifist;
but he objected to capitalist wars and saw no point in this one. He
carried on the fight against war wherever he could. In June 1918, at
the state convention of the Ohio Socialist party, he carried the fight
too far. Speaking with old-time defiance, he paid his tribute to the

Socialists arrested under the Espionage Act. Four days later he was indicted for violating the law himself.

They charged him with uttering words intended to cause insubordination and disloyalty within the military forces of tthe United States, to incite resistance to the war, and to promote the cause of Germany. In a last speech to the jury Debs stated an eloquent case. "I admit being opposed to the present form of government," he said. "I admit being opposed to the present social system. I am doing what little I can, and have been for many years, to bring about a change that shall do away with the rule of the great body of the people by a relatively small group and establish in this country an industrial and social democracy. . . . What you may choose to do to me will be of small consequence. . . . American institutions are on trial here before a court of American citizens."

The court of American citizens may perhaps be excused for its hysteria when one reflects how wide the infection spread. Woodrow Wilson was among those who would not forgive Debs. . . .

A jury of his fellow-citizens convicted Debs; and the Supreme Court, in an opinion by Justice Oliver Wendell Holmes, sustained the conviction. In April 1919, the old man, broken in health but still indomitable in spirit, prepared to serve a ten-year sentence. Socialists throughout the country still looked to him as their leader; and the 1920 Socialist party convention nominated convict #9653 at Atlanta for president of the United States. The choice, someone said, was between Debs and dubs. Warren G. Harding won over the Democrat James M. Cox, Debs polling over 900,000 votes.

Some kindly fellow-instinct of midwestern democracy must have given the new Republican president a sympathy with Debs which Wilson, the scholar and liberal, never had. Toward the end of 1921 Harding ordered Debs's release. "We understand each other perfectly," Debs said after a visit to the White House. Then the old Socialist returned to Terre Haute.

The Russian Revolution had meanwhile split anew the already splintered Socialists. Debs had exulted in the first reports of the October Revolution. He wrote, "From the crown of my head to the soles of my feet I am Bolshevik, and proud of it." But the formation of what is now called the Communist party troubled him. "It has been the fate of our movement from the beginning especially in this country, to split," he wrote from Atlanta. "About the time we get in shape to do something we have to split up and waste our energy in factional strife. We preach unity everlastingly, but we ourselves keep splitting apart."

Debs was sixty-six on his release, an ill and weary man. The new

Russia perplexed him. In 1922 he protested the Communist persecutions of the Social Revolutionaries. "Soviet Russia can set an example," he cabled Lenin, "by refusing to follow the practices of worldwide Czardom, and should uphold the higher standards we seek to erect and profess to observe." Yet a few months later he could write that, no matter "what its mistakes have been, nor what may be charged against it, the Russian revolution . . . is the greatest, most luminous and far-reaching achievement in the entire sweep of human history."

Debs came to object increasingly to the Communist International. "When they proceed to dictate to the Socialist parties of other countries as to how they should conduct themselves," he said, "then it seems to me to be the time to back up." And he had little use for the American Communist party, then in its underground phase. "Any underground radical movement in the United States is not only foolish, but suicidal." He resented the indifference with which the Communists had regarded his years in Atlanta. "So far as they were concerned," Theodore Debs wrote bitterly to the editor of the *Daily Worker,* " 'Gene would still be rotting in his dungeon." When he saw that the decision could not be avoided, he identified himself with the Socialist party.

He pressed ahead in his work, writing on the need for prison reform, working for the party, till fatigue would overtake him and send him, ashen-gray and trembling, to his bed or to Lindlahr, the Socialist sanitarium in Chicago. In the 1924 presidential campaign, he concurred in the Socialist endorsement of Robert M. La Follette. Two years later, on October 20, 1926, a quiet event in the bustle of Republican prosperity, Eugene V. Debs died.

There passed away with Debs a great American democrat. The radical passions of the Jacksonians, the Free Soilers, the Populists spoke through Debs—only now in the unaccustomed vocabulary of Socialism. *"The capitalist class! The working class! The class struggle!"* Debs would cry. "These are the supreme economic and political facts of this day and the precise terms that express them." Yet, for all the violence of his Socialist rhetoric, Debs held firmly to democratic traditions of change through debate and consent. Some sure intuition made him avoid the syndicalist terrorism of the IWW or the conspiratorial disloyalties of the American Communist party. Every man's good neighbor in Terre Haute, the advocate of home and mother, the admirer of Tom Mix, the man who understood Harding, the friend of Riley and Field and later of Carl Sandburg and Sinclair Lewis, Debs had American instincts too deeply ingrained in him. Though as a pre-Soviet Socialist he never had to face squarely the ambiguities which the USSR has revealed in collectivism, his essential faith in the free play of political life was already stirring him to uneasy protest. Socialism could never again be so simple as it was before the First World War.

Debs saw many things too simply. He underestimated the American middle class and the vitality of American capitalism. His own career disproved his repeated assertion that capitalism would destroy political freedom. Yet, in the central fight of American democracy— the fight against the political aspirations of the business community —Debs played an honorable and significant role. "In my humble opinion," writes his old comrade-in-arms, George H. Goebel, "those years of education forced on the people, in towns big and little (from pulpit, platform and soapbox, by voice, leaflet and books), saved this country from civil war in the depths of depression, and gave Franklin D. Roosevelt . . . the understanding public and trained workers for the immediate job he had on taking over."

H. Wayne Morgan:
Debs, Successful Advocate
of an Unsuccessful Cause[1]

Debs greatly disliked party gatherings and did his best to rise above factions. He had no stomach for doctrinal haggling and no will to fight socialists. He much preferred the color, glamor, and excitement of the lecture circuit to the convention hall or planning board. He felt uncomfortable in the midst of theorists, yet he himself in his way fashioned a social philosophy which was a curious blend of American and European doctrine, of individualism and collectivism, of idealism and realism.

In truth he knew little of the academic theories of socialism or the formal discipline of Marx or other socialist thinkers, but the goal for which he strove was the same as theirs and, once converted to socialism, he accepted the basic tenets of the creed without reservation. Early in his career as a socialist he founded his social theory on a few principles to which he adhered throughout his life. . . .

He believed that industrial capitalism and the profit motive it insured were the roots of all evil, for they created a system which oppressed the individual and enabled some men to profit unjustly from the labor of others. If capitalism could be replaced by a more humane cooperative socialism, the whole social system, the very nature of man and his world, could be changed for the better. A basic paradox in all of Debs's thinking was his quest for greater individual freedom and development through the adoption of an equalitarian cooperative society.

This belief that capitalism was evil and in a transitional phase motivated Debs's attack on the economic system of his day. "The day of individual effort, of small tools, free competition, hand labor, long hours and meager results is gone never to return," he said bluntly in 1904. "The civilization reared upon this old foundation is crumbling." Men were bad because the system was bad; he was an environmentalist of the simplest type. For that reason he did not hate the capitalist, for he, like the worker, was merely a product of the system. "We shouldn't forget that many capitalists are born capitalists

[1] From H. Wayne Morgan, *Eugene V. Debs: Socialist For President* (Syracuse, N.Y.: Syracuse University Press, 1962), pp. 21–25, 199–205. Copyright © 1962 by Syracuse University Press. Reprinted by permission of the publisher.

just as many workers are born workers, and the former are creatures of their environment and circumstance in precisely the same sense as the latter." Change the system and you change the men, that was his answer.

His personal sentimentality and his wish to believe in his fellow men blended with a genuine belief in the goodness of men to raise his theory to an exalted vision. "Love and labor in alliance, working together, have transforming, redeeming, and emancipating power," he said. "Under their benign sway the world can be made better and brighter." . . .

Debs devoted his whole career to agitating for a revolution which never came but in which he never lost faith. A second paradox of his thinking was his distrust of violence though he preached revolution. In truth, there was little substance to the menacing shadows cast by his revolutionary talk, for he believed that socialism could and would be adopted through the ballot in America; he never envisaged an upheaval comparable to the Russian Revolution. His steadfast belief in socialist political action rested upon the assumption that once the workers were aroused and educated, they would vote socialism into being. "[The Ballot] can give our civilization its crowning glory—the cooperative commonwealth." He was radical in the end he wished to attain more than in the means by which he wished to attain it. If anything, he was representative of a generation of American reformers who sought revolutionary ends by orderly and peaceful means. His reliance on common sense, education, the ballot instead of the bullet, placed him in the mainstream of American radicalism.

The coming commonwealth was real to him, as it was to other dedicated socialists of the day, and he believed in what he taught. Man could be made new again, the world could be made beautiful. . . . If Debs was aware of the contradictions, the naïveté, the lack of realism in his social theories he did not admit it; in fact, he probably reflected little upon them. He spoke his beliefs for all to hear, not asking that they agree, asking only that they understand. It was easy for him to cling to his ideals for he participated little in the party organization, had almost nothing to do with party doctrine, and spent most of his time among people who agreed with him and who were easily swayed by his words. His mission was to evangelize socialism, to verbalize as one the protest of many, to be the Great Agitator of his day. . . .

Debs came to American socialism at a time when it needed his qualities most. He gave to it his color, enthusiasm, boundless energy, and American ideals. He became a figure around whom socialists of every stripe could rally in times of crisis. He brought a national reputation and important connections with the labor movement and the common people. The socialists could indeed be proud of having captured his allegiance. He was one with his new comrades in the belief that the future belonged to socialism. . . .

Debs was not so remarkable for the way he worked, in which he differed little from many contemporaries, as for the effectiveness with which he preached socialism. If his means differed little from those of other politicians of his day, his goals did, and that he persuaded nearly 6 percent of the voting Americans in 1912 to mark their ballots for him was no small accomplishment.

Yet, because they recognized his basic Americanism and because he was at such pains to disavow the more extreme socialist tendencies even if it displeased his comrades, the Americans who voted for him did not fear him. His belief in the goodness of man and his personal sentimentality tempered whatever edge of violence remained on the doctrines he spoke. Knowing little of formal socialist logic he was indebted to no theorizer or dogmatist for his doctrines.

This in part explains his remarkable effectiveness with the voting public of his day, for he cast doctrine and theory aside, like most good politicians, and fitted his remarks and his program into the mainstream of the time. He appealed to many different groups successfully because he realized that to be effective any political doctrine, even idealistic socialism, must be understood by its audience. Thus he avoided extended philosophical discussions, preferring the concrete realities of the life around him to sophistry.

However wise this may have been in terms of gathering votes and followers, it is one measure of Debs's weakness as a leader that he did not fully grasp the elements of socialist theory and use them in his leadership. He was not, strictly speaking, a socialist party leader yet he was the most famous socialist of his day. Characteristically, he preferred to leave control of the party, with all its bitter dissension and routine labor, to others while he himself used his talents to rally popular opinion for what he considered the party program. From his point of view it was wise to remain above faction that he might be a true leader above the battle to whom all socialists could look for leadership. Yet in doing so he permitted the party organization to drift into the firm control of men with whom he disagreed, while he could not wholeheartedly join the men with whom he agreed. Thus, like many radical leaders, he was perpetually between two fires, radical socialism and evolutionary socialism. Had he chosen to exercise the power represented by his following he no doubt could have dominated the party, yet by doing so he would have risked his neutral position and the formation of yet another faction. The loosely organized party, composed of varied elements prone to disagreement, was hard to govern at best and Debs disliked the formality and procedures of such rule as much as the methods of obtaining them.

If he did not fully exercise his talents for leadership within the party he did so outside the party organization. As the best-known socalist of his day, and recognizing his role as the prophet and evangelizer of socialism, he lent his talents to spreading the meaning if not the formal doctrines of American socialism. His career was varied, though it flowed from the same central source; he worked as a labor organizer, protest leader, socialist propagandizer, and as a symbol of freedom in a time of oppression. In his role as a presidential candidate he brought to bear all his understanding of the temper of the times, of human nature, and of the political system in which he worked. His idealism did not prevent him from being a shrewd judge of character and men, and he understood mass psychology as well as or better than any other political leader of his day. Debs's political career illustrates the curious blending of intellectual and emotional idealism and practical realism so common to liberal politics in America. On the one hand he sincerely believed in the utopian idealism he preached; on the other hand he knew full well that his new order could be attained only by working within the exisiting system. This was a wise and profound understanding on his part, and it is the measure of his familiarity with the political habits of his countrymen. Thus he eschewed violence not only because he himself could not justify it but because he knew it would ruin his chances of success with the American people.

Debs's presidential campaigns were important to the Socialist party for they focused the strength of socialism every four years. Furthermore, Debs's evangelizing and his popularity with the sympathetic masses to whom he appealed added new members to the rolls, stimulated the party press, brought others to work for socialism and illustrated to those in doubt the vigor of the movement. Debs, acutely aware of this, missed no chance to add to the party strength by appealing to labor, seeking members, and doing organizational work.

The Socialist party greatly benefited from the progressive temper in the years between 1901 and 1914, but it also profited from its own hard work with the masses. It had a genuine appeal to the educated middle class, and though Debs himself deplored the middle-class trend in the party after 1908, he could do little to arrest it. In fact, organized labor did not vote the socialist ticket except when it knew that socialism had no chance of winning; this in turn drove many socialists to the middle class for support. The failure to win organized labor sealed socialism's doom as a growing political force in America.

The socialist movement as a whole suffered from many more defects than its failure to win organized labor. Its loose organization, while a blessing to much of the membership, prevented the discipline and unity of European socialist parties. Debs himself would have been the last to sanction such discipline and though he perpetually called for socialist unity he based that unity on principles, rather than organizational discipline. The internal factions which arose in the party in its golden age contributed greatly to its decline, yet in the end were only part of a multitude of factors working against its success.

In the last analysis, the American socialist movement failed to conquer capitalism and its society for deeper reasons than internal strife. The unexpected vitality of capitalism, the immovable middle-class psychology of workers, the truly basic American belief in individual rather than cooperative effort, the conservative constitutional features of the political system, and the antisocialism of organized labor which prevented a broadly-based coalition labor party—these deeply woven threads in the fabric of American life prevented socialism's triumph.

Yet American socialism's ultimate failure is not so impressive as its temporary success. The people who voted for Debs five times apparently believed in many of his ideals; the party elevated several hundred of its members to office; undeniably socialism influenced the older parties in their search for reform measures. . . . Thus the party fulfilled the historic role of third parties in the American system—it attained enough success with the people to force older parties to steal its thunder. Despite its idealism and seemingly un-American approach to the problems of the day, the Socialist party gained more success with the voters than any other recent third party except the Populists. . . .

None gave more to that movement than Eugene Victor Debs. If he was often beset by doubts, if he often vacillated on momentous issues, if he partially failed in his role as a leader within the Socialist party, and if his thinking was indeed shallow, he was no less effective. He appealed frankly to the people whom he understood in terms they understood and let others in the movement explain the fine points. Though he wore his romantic idealism like a crusading knight capitalizing on every gain to be made from the dramatic role, his sincerity was above question. He did in truth believe that socialism was inevitable, and that its inauguration would mean the rule of reason and love on earth. He suffered for his beliefs, yet did not abandon them. Twice imprisoned, once as an old man, he nonetheless clung to his ideals. "I do not consider that I have made any sacrifice whatever," he said early in his career, "no man does, unless he violates his conscience." At the end of the road he might well have repeated that phrase, for indeed he had not violated his own.

Ray Ginger: Debs's Failures and Strengths[1]

When Eugene Debs helped to establish the Industrial Workers of the World in 1905, he selected a method that defeated his own purpose. Debs and his colleagues conceived of the IWW as a powerful instrument in the campaign for industrial unions. They confidently expected that the IWW would soon demonstrate its superiority over the craft unions, and that the majority of craft unionists would rally to the standard of the New Unionism. This failed to happen for several reasons: the employers made concessions to the AFL, but fought viciously against the IWW. Many workers had a financial stake in the insurance funds of the established unions, and they were unwilling to sacrifice these benefits. The workers' own sense of labor solidarity drove them into the largest federation, the AFL, and mere habit tended to keep them there. The AFL knew the importance of stable locals, signed contracts, and control of working conditions.

Thus the formation of the IWW tended to delay rather than to promote the campaign for industrial unions and socialism. Eugene Debs always argued that the labor movement should strive for the complete destruction of the wage system. But in 1905, by his own action, he isolated himself from the great majority of the organized workers, who stilled clung to the AFL. The leaders of the AFL denied everything that Debs affirmed. Samuel Gompers was not merely a craft unionist; he also bitterly opposed the theory that the labor movement should fight for socialism or any other ultimate goal. His program was based on the improvement of living standards within the capitalist framework: More; Here; Now. Inadvertently, Debs had delivered the basic organization of the workingmen, the trade unions, into the grip of Gompers' philosophy.

The example of his own American Railway Union doubtless inclined Eugene Debs toward the IWW, but the two cases were not the same. Only tortured reasoning could call the ARU a dual union. The ARU came into being because the established brotherhoods had failed to organize many railroads who were eager for organization. . . .

The real reason behind Debs's infatuation with dual unionism was not related to the ARU. Eugene Debs considered every question in

[1] From Ray Ginger, *Eugene V. Debs: The Making of an American Radical* (New York: Macmillan Co., 1962), pp. 273–78, 397, 480–82. Originally published as *The Bending Cross* (New Brunswick, N.J.: Rutgers University Press, 1949). Reprinted by permission of Rutgers University Press.

terms of the working class against the capitalist class, and he absolutely refused to compromise with his chosen enemy. . . . Debs did not try to destroy the AFL, and he always supported its strikes. He merely refused to join it, refused to try to change it from within, refused to dirty his hands by contact with Samuel Gompers' federation. As he commented in his letter to the *Social Democratic Herald*: "I have simply joined a trade union that suits me. That's all."

In several other instances, Debs chose a method that defeated his goal. Each of these mistakes stemmed from his habit of regarding every question as a "purely class question." Thus, even though the party could have gained members and spread its doctrines by participation in several reform movements, Debs always refused to cooperate with any reform party to achieve a limited objective. . . . This policy caused the party to miss many opportunities to educate workingmen outside its ranks, but the party's attitude toward the Negro people was even more shortsighted.

Many leaders of the Socialist party, either consciously or unconsciously, had ill-concealed prejudice toward Negroes. . . . Eugene Debs's attitude on this question was quite different. His numerous organizing trips through the South had convinced him that white workingmen would be exploited so long as the Negroes were held in an inferior position. . . . Debs always refused to speak before segregated audiences. In several cases he threatened to cancel engagements rather than yield to local prejudice.

Debs's firm stand against racial prejudice was not solely due to general good will. He was convinced that any racial or religious division was harmful to the entire labor movement. . . . When he did encounter discrimination against Negroes, Debs's wrath fairly boiled over. . . . Debs soon received . . . an anonymous letter, which predicted that the Socialists would "lose more votes than you think" if they insisted on equality for the Negroes. The letter was signed, "A staunch member of the Socialist party." Debs printed this advice . . . and furiously replied that the party "would be false to its historic mission, violate the fundamental principles of Socialism, deny its philosophy and repudiate its own teachings if, on account of race considerations, it sought to exclude any human being from political and economic freedom."

But Debs refused to concede that poor Negroes were in a worse position than poor white people. When the party convention of 1903 resolved to make a special fight for the rights of Negroes, Debs opposed the action. . . . Debs then argued: "We have nothing special to offer the Negro, and we cannot make separate appeals to all the races. The Socialist party is the party of the whole working class, regardless of color—the whole working class of the whole world."

So the Socialist party, immobilized by Victor Berger's prejudice and Debs's oversimplified analysis, failed to adopt a specialized program for the Negro people. When race prejudice was thrust at Debs, he always publicly repudiated it. He always insisted on absolute equality. But he failed to accept the view that special measures were sometimes needed to achieve this equality. After Debs had decided that the main problem was the emancipation of the workingman, he refused to be concerned with lesser problems, although he himself had argued that white workers would never be free so long as Negroes were oppressed.

Debs's beliefs on dual unionism, cooperation with reform parties, and the problems of the Negro people, all flowed from a common source. He was determined to hew to a revolutionary program and not be diverted by reform movements. If his mind failed to grasp a direct connection between a proposed reform and socialism, he refused to waste time with the reform. Then argument became futile; he could not be swayed. . . . Always willing to concede his fallibility on minor issues, he went his own way on basic policy. In each case he sought justification in that most private of all places, his conscience. . . . His conscience was the Great Umpire, and Debs was the only spectator near enough to hear the umpire's decisions. . . .

But in spite of these faults Eugene Debs deserves to be known as the political leader of American socialism. He clung with stubborn insistence to the basic principles of Marxian socialism. He showed an uncanny ability to foresee issues and to devise remedies. He first raised the standard against the prosecution of Bill Haywood and Fred Warren and the McNamaras; against intervention in Mexico; against participation in the [First] World War. He played a part in hundreds of hard-fought strikes. He hurled his waning energies into the struggle for American recognition of Soviet Russia. Debs's sole purpose was to inspire a working-class revolt against the capitalist system, and his success was truly remarkable. He kindled the fires of a newer hope for millions of his fellow citizens.

And through all of these temporary battles, Debs held to the twin objectives that he had announced before 1900, industrial unionism and revolutionary politics. No other prominent radical was entitled to the same boast. The right wing of the party had become enamored with reform platforms and machine methods; the left wing had sought the illusory success of anarcho-syndicalism; Debs had staunchly opposed both trends. He had consistently been among the first to capitalize on immediate issues, and he had never forgotten his ultimate goal of socialism. Debs's career is startling, not because he made mistakes, but because he made so few of them. . . .

Few Americans stood apart from the national sorrow at the death of Eugene Debs. The audience at his funeral included famous writers, wealthy attorneys and businessmen, ordinary men with the grease of a lifetime ground into their thumbnails. Each of these mourners created an idol in his own image. Some found in Eugene Debs a misguided zealot who nonetheless was sincere and charitable. Others admired the Socialist leader because of his pioneer work for woman suffrage, social-security legislation, industrial unionism, the extension of civil liberties.

So it became fashionable to minimize his radical beliefs in favor of his purity of character. On this count he was deemed above reproach. . . . From his observations of American life he arrived at a specific solution. His conclusion held that the common people were being crucified by an outmoded economic system. On the accuracy of that belief must rest the ultimate worth of his career. The admonition to love one another, which dominated his early thinking, he characterized in 1919 as "a harmless doctrine." He had come to believe that devotion to the oppressed must be shown by resistance to the oppressors. This contention that modern society holds two social classes, two conflicting interests, lay at the root of his entire program.

This process of change from Christian to Marxist was never completed by Eugene Debs, and it cast up grave inconsistencies in his temperament. While some of his talents flourished, others were static, still others atrophied. His gifts as an agitator and his feeling for social realities were matched by a gross ignorance of science, literature, all fields of scholarship. His activities were rife with contradictions, with petty foibles, with mistakes both minor and serious. But it is difficult to speak with confidence of the faults of Eugene Debs. . . .

Hence the story of Eugene Debs becomes the story of a whole generation of wage earners and dirt farmers. While these people learned something from the Socialist leader, he learned even more from them. His awesome strength in time of crisis was made possible by his confidence in his fellows. At such moments his finite self seemed to merge with the agonized wanderings of the nameless multitude. Out of these popular yearnings and struggles the mind of Eugene Debs fashioned a supreme maxim: Human happiness is never found by a solitary search. No man rises far above the ranks.

Bert Cochran:
The Achievement of Debs[1]

Eugene V. Debs can unquestionably be considered the spiritual father of the Socialist party which was formally founded in Indianapolis in 1901, and which stood at the forefront of American radicalism for the next twenty years. There is no question that he was the most popular and effective socialist figure ever to appear in America. No one in this time, or since, has even remotely approached him in his impact on the American people. He struck a spark wherever he went, and was the only American left-wing leader around whom a *personal legend* grew up, in the manner of famed rebels of old. Is he simply to be admired and honored as a colorful personality and America's first great socialist apostle, or is there, beyond that, something in his life and work that can guide those of us who are seeking to recreate American socialism as a mass movement?

. . . Debs combined an overwhelming sympathy and sense of comradeship for his fellow man with the burning zeal and uncompromising resolve of the indomitable revolutionist. . . . Debs not only was a revolutionist: he was completely conscious of what was involved when he chose that road. "Hold Your Nerve" was the significant title of an article he wrote for the *Appeal to Reason* in 1907, in which he talked about the revolutionist's way of life. Ferdinand Lassalle, the brilliant social revolutionist, once said that "the war against capitalism was not a rosewater affair. . . . It is rather of the storm and tempest order. . . . All kinds of attacks must be expected, and all kinds of wounds will be inflicted. . . . You will be assailed within and without, spat upon by the very ones that you are doing your best to serve, and at certain crucial moments find yourself isolated, absolutely alone as if to compel surernder, but in those moments, if you have the nerve, you become supreme."

. . . Eugene Debs preached a militant class-struggle brand of socialism. He was a champion of fighting industrial unionism and, in the initial days of its formation, lent his efforts to building the IWW. As a lecturer and agitator, and for many years as chief editorial writer for the *Appeal to Reason,* he was in the forefront of every important

[1] From Bert Cochran, "The Achievement of Debs," in Harvey Goldberg, ed., *American Radicals, Some Problems and Personalities* (New York: Monthly Review Press, 1957), pp. 163–64, 166–67, 168–70, 171–73, 174, 176. Reprinted by permission of Monthly Review Press.

labor battle of that period, whether it was a strike, a free-speech contest, an organizing campaign, an election, or the defense of a framed labor organizer. . . .

Debs was the most influential single leader through the two decades when socialism constituted an important movement, and he was generally accepted as its main spokesman. . . . At the 1912 convention, just six months before Debs's greatest campaign triumph, Hillquit and Berger and the other party officials crushed the left wing, and soon afterwards drove its leader, Haywood, and thousands of his followers out of the party. How explain the anomaly that socialism's leading spokesman had so little influence inside his own party?

Here we come to a peculiar side of Debs's makeup. Some of the very qualities which made him the irresistible personality that he was, conspired to make it impossible for him to assume the burdens of party organization leader. . . . He made up his mind in those early days to stay out of all these internal conflicts and keep himself free to do his big work. He thereafter went to such extremes that for twenty years he never participated in a party convention, never ran for or held a party position, never attempted to line up members behind his views, and never took part in the left wing's organizational deliberations. . . .

[As a result, in 1912] the revolutionary socialists were deprived of the considerable support that Debs could have swung behind their faction had he been so disposed. Moreover, by abdicating as a political leader in this matter, he was able to exert little influence in shaping the character of the left wing. And this was a pity, because the revolutionary elements were then sidetracked by syndicalism and by mistaken notions about "direct action." They could have been straightened out by Debs, who had a better feel of the American labor movement, and a superior understanding of the all-round nature of the political struggle for socialism. For Debs was one of the very few prominent Socialists who consistently steered clear of both opportunist and syndicalist misconceptions. But since he kept himself aloof, the struggles between the two factions developed along the lines of reformism versus a revolutionary socialism vitiated by syndicalism. . . .

In recent years, Debs has been criticized from a different point of view. William Z. Foster and others have found fault with the great agitator for his dual unionism, his opposition to a labor party, and his underestimation of the Negro question. . . . With the exception of the last point, the criticisms are, I think, not well taken. . . .

It is more than doubtful that Debs can properly be criticized for having abandoned the Railroad Brotherhoods and launching the American Railway Union in 1893. The organization was not the dream child of some radicals but rather the product of the actual experiences of the railroad workers. It was headed by some of the most prominent rail unionists of that period. And proof of its validity was the fact that in a year's time the ARU had more members than all the Brotherhoods put together. . . .

The founding of the IWW in 1905 by left-wing socialists is a more debatable proposition. But even this is not the clear-cut mistake that Ray Ginger imagines it to be. The AFL had a membership of less than a million and a half in 1905, and was moreover bound by a gentleman's understanding with the National Civic Federation to confine itself to the thin stratum of skilled crafts, thus in effect abandoning the mass of unskilled workers. It is by no means established that an independent industrial union movement might not have prospered at that time. Where Debs, Haywood, and the other left-wingers erred was in their equation of industrial unionism with revolutionary politics, making the IWW into a red revolutionary organization with all the trimmings. The IWW might have had mass appeal as a straightforward movement for modern unionism, but as a cross between a union and a revolutionary party its appeal was decidedly limited. . . .

The labor party criticism has the appearance of an attempt mistakenly to transplant the conditions and problems of the present to those of Debs's day. From 1901 to World War I, the Socialist party was the biggest labor political organization on the scene. The isolated attempts of some local unions here and there to form local labor parties represented diversionary movements from the mainstream rather than possibilities of organizing the labor political movement on a broader basis. . . .

On the Negro question, the Socialist party is open to strong condemnation. The party sucked up the prejudices of middle-class America and was rife with Jim Crow attitudes. Debs fought these chauvinistic manifestations with his customary vigor, but he believed that it all reduced itself to the labor question. He did not understand the responsibility of socialists to champion the specific fight for Negro equality. . . .

Debs's right-wing opponents maintained that he was no leader at all. As the party's internal struggles grew fiercer, the officials got the word around that his heart was bigger than his head. . . . But Debs held firm to Marxist *principles* throughout his life as a socialist, which could not be said of the Rand School scholars and theorists. Beyond that, he had a profound knowledge of the American labor movement, and an uncanny instinct for what was right. Despite his individualistic habits and his aloofness from inner-party conflicts he undoubtedly was the national spokesman of American socialism in its halcyon period. His tactical sense was exceptionally keen, his kinship with the American worker was extraordinarily close and sensitive, and he understood better than anybody else the meaning and content of a broad, all-national, political struggle for the minds and hearts of the American people. He was the first to blaze the trail for industrial unionism. He was the first to raise the standard against the prosecutions of William Haywood, Fred Warren, and the McNamara brothers. He crowned his work with the dramatic demonstration against the war, first in his Canton speech, and again in the courtroom. . . . His conception of a broad struggle for socialism, undominated by machine politics, opportunism, or bureaucratism, retains its validity. And it can further be avowed that some of Debs's incomparable virtues which captured the American imagination will be sought again in the socialist leaders to come, and that the chords which he struck in the American heart, of human solidarity and the passion for honesty, straightforwardness, and fair play, will have to be struck again if a new emancipatory movement of national proportions is to be called forth.

David Herreshoff:
Debs, Exponent of
De Leonist Unionism[1]

The Socialist party was full of traditional American radicalism. . . . There was also a De Leonist influence which made itself felt chiefly through Debs. . . . The political fact was that former SLP members who joined the SP as a rule were pro-AFL as well as anti-De Leon. But Debs since 1893 had opposed craft and promoted industrial unionism. His American Railway Union was dual to the railroad craft organizations. . . . But just how close to the politics of the SLP did Debs come? Let us take the testimony of Debs and De Leon themselves on this point.

In 1905 at the founding convention of the IWW, Debs had this to say about his relations with De Leon:

> We have not been the best of friends in the past (laughter), but the whirligig of time brings about some wonderful changes. I find myself breaking away from some men I have been in very close touch with, and getting in close touch with some men from whom I have been widely separated.

Debs, it is clear from this, was well aware that support for the IWW and collaboration with De Leon would involve strife with other leaders of the SP, in particular those with AFL connections. Nevertheless Debs persisted in his course, though not to the point of split with the center and right wings of the SP. Two essays contributed by Debs to the *International Socialist Review* in 1912 and 1914 show the continuing closeness of Debs's standpoint to De Leon's. In the first of these two articles Debs was trying to ward off a split in the SP between the pro-IWW left and the pro-AFL center and right. He pleaded for an authentic American socialism which would devise tactics without respect to "the precedents of other countries. We have to develop our own and they must be adapted to the American people and to American conditions." Debs knew, as De Leon realized in 1908, that there was no immediate prospect of concensus on tactics. "We are in for a

[1] From David Herreshoff, *American Disciples of Marx: From the Age of Jackson to the Progressive Era* (Detroit, Wayne State University Press, 1967), pp. 181–86. Reprinted by permission of the author and Wayne State University Press. Copyright 1967 by Wayne State University Press.

lively time at the very best before we work out these differences and settle down to a policy of united and constructive work for Socialism instead of spending so much time and energy lampooning one another."

Like the De Leon who lined himself to Thomas Skidmore, Debs repudiated bourgeois property rights. "As a revolutionist I can have no respect for capitalist property laws, nor the least scruple about violating them. I hold such laws to have been enacted through chicanery, fraud, and corruption, with the sole end of dispossessing, robbing, and enslaving the working class." Also, like De Leon, is Debs's dissociation from the Wobblies' verbal cult of violence:

> There have been times in the past, and there are countries today where the frenzied deed of a glorious fanatic like old John Brown seems to have been inspired by Jehovah himself, but I am now dealing with the twentieth century and with the United States.

Under American conditions, Debs continued, "a great body of organized workers, such as the Socialist movement, cannot predicate its tactical procedure upon such exceptional instances" as those which might justify resort to violence. As with De Leon, so with Debs the key to nonviolent revolution was consciousness: "To the extent that the working class has power based on its class-consciousness, force is unnecessary; to the extent that power is lacking, force can only result in harm." To those IWW leaders who toyed with the idea of substituting force for mass support Debs spoke of the need to work "in the broad open light of day. Nothing can be done by stealth that can be of advantage in this country. . . . The American workers are law-abiding and no amount of sneering or derision will alter that fact." If the IWW "ignores political action, or treats it with contempt by advising the workers to 'strike at the ballot box with an ax,' they will regard it as an anarchist organization, and it will never be more than a small fraction of the labor movement."

Debs was more flexible than De Leon customarily was when he urged "industrial independent organization, especially among the millions who have not yet been organized at all" while simultaneously advocating "the 'boring from within' for all that can be accomplished by industrial unionists in the craft unions." But he was just as unbending as De Leon in his attitude toward the AFL bureaucracy: "The Socialist party cannot be neutral on the union question. . . . I am opposed under all circumstances to any party alliances or affiliations with reactionary trade unions." This attitude was connected with the De Leonist stress he placed on the importance of class-consciousness: "The sound education of the workers and their thorough organization, both economic and political, on the basis of the class struggle, must precede their emancipation."

In 1913 Debs wrote "A Plea for Solidarity" in which he urged reunification of the syndicalist majority and the De Leonist minority of the IWW on the basis of the De Leonist program that was "cornerstoned in the true principles of unionism in reference to political action." In the same article he sought to unify the SP and the SLP and expressed the conviction that unity of socialists on the industrial and political fields would produce in America "the foremost proletarian revolutionary movement in the world."

In retrospection a few months before his death in 1914, De Leon gauged his closeness to Debs. He recalled that after the split of 1899 the anti-De Leon SLP members "fled for asylum to the political movement that Eugene V. Debs had just started in the west." Toward the Debs movement De Leon had been "hopefully expectant":

> Debs was no AF of L man. Far otherwise and to the contrary. He had no superstitious horror for "rival" or "dual" unions; nor did he entertain any superstitious reverence for "boring from within." If the structure of an economic organization was wrong and there was no other way to mend matters, he believed in setting up another union, and he boldly practiced what he preached. What is more, he rose to prominence as a leader of just such practices. Indeed, it was at the time, and even since then off and on, hard to tell Debs from the SLP so far as the union question was concerned. The expectation seemed justified that the political movement which Debs conjured into existence as a leader in the formation of revolutionary unions, would be animated by his breath. As a consequence, it was expected that the seceders from the SLP would be captured by the political asylum to which they fled. As a further consequence, it was hoped and even expected in 1900, and the expectation rearose in 1905 when the IWW was launched with the joint assistance of Debs and the SLP, that AF of Lism would be uprooted. It all happened the other way. The seceders from the SLP captured their political asylum; the AF of L was "saved."

It was a paradox to which Debs himself bowed that he, the most attractive and persuasive of leaders, was not a maker of policy for the SP. Debs elected to carry on an energetic propaganda before the broadest public he could reach but declined to take part in the factional infighting of the SP. This die of his political behavior must be contrasted to De Leon's. Perhaps Debs's reputation for benevolence depended on his refusal to fight with the determination of a De Leon to persuade the SP to adopt his tactics. Debs had justified factional ruthlessness at the IWW's founding convention. "A man," he had said "is not worthy, in my judgment, to enlist in the services of the working class unless he has the moral stamina, if need be, to break asunder all personal relations to serve that class." But Debs did not subsequently perform according to the code he then sanctioned. There was in Debs a rare combination of fiery militancy and fraternity; he synthesized a near-De Leonist Marxism with the practice of brotherhood:

> We need above all the real Socialist spirit, which expresses itself in boundless enthusiasm, energetic action, and the courage to dare and do all things in the service of the cause. We need to *be* comrades in all the term implies and to help and cheer and strengthen one another in the daily struggle. If the "love of comrades" is but a barren ideality in the Socialist movement, then there is no place for it in the heart of mankind.

The fraternal Debs had passed into legend. It would be well if the legend could incorporate the fact that the fraternal Debs was also the revolutionary man of action who went to the country with the De Leonist version of Marxism and evoked a greater response than has yet come to another American labor radical. It must be that he was important for his ideas as well as for himself.

James Weinstein:
The Limits of Postwar
Debsian Socialism[1]

When Eugene V. Debs ran for president of the United States for the first time, in 1900, the Socialist party had not yet formally been organized. Yet in his person Debs almost perfectly represented the new party then coming together. That party, the old Socialist Party of America, formed as a coalition of several tendencies and regional groups. Among these were the Social Democratic party, of which Debs and Victor Berger were leaders; a section of the Socialist Labor party, led by Morris Hillquit; Christian Socialists; former Populists; and Western miners. In short, the formation of the Socialist party was the result of a confluence of the major socialist and radical tendencies that had grown up during the social turmoil of the 1890s, and marked a coming of age for the anticapitalist movement in the United States. As it began, so it remained during the years of its growth and vitality: a party of substantial internal diversity and open and democratic structure. From 1901 to 1912 the party grew rapidly; until the split of 1919 it retained its basic character and strength.

Debs's role within the party was unique in that he alone could speak unashamedly in the name of virtually the entire membership. His presidential nominations in four of the five election years from 1900 to 1920 were the result of neither accident nor organizational influence—Debs held no office in the party structure throughout these years. Rather, they were the results of his own experience and of the party's heterogeneity. Other leaders of the party, particularly its most articulate and able organization men and women, represented their own sections of the party. Berger, for example, was popular in Wisconsin but was heartily disliked by those party members opposed to the building of solid electoral machinery or to working within the American Federation of Labor. Hillquit, who led the New York party, was widely distrusted by most of the same groups. The Christian Socialists, in turn, had little rapport with those in Milwaukee or New York, while the former Populists aspired primarily to build the party locally—which meant in Texas and Oklahoma, primarily. Other party leaders who were known nationally—the journalists like Charles Edward

[1] This article was written expressly for this volume. Copyright 1970 by James Weinstein.

Russell, John Spargo, Algie M. Simons, or William English Walling—
could never speak for the whole party because of their distance from
its industrial-working-class and tenant-farmer base. IWW Socialists, although they had a following that cut across regional or group lines,
increasingly opposed political action and engaged in dual-union activities rejected by most of the membership. For a short period of time—
from 1908 to 1912—William D. Haywood emerged as a party leader
with a broad base among diverse sections of the membership, but as the
IWW and the party diverged Haywood stood with the IWW and was
removed from the National Executive Committee of the party in 1913.

In contrast, Debs was strongly identified with no single section of
the party but could speak for all. He had come to Socialism via the
Woodstock jail and the ruins of the American Railway Union, which
he had organized with great success and which had been destroyed by
the federal government during the Pullman strike of 1894. Before he
organized the ARU, Debs had been the secretary-treasurer of the
Brotherhood of Locomotive Firemen and editor of its journal from
1880 to 1892. During these years he had been elected city clerk of
Terre Haute and a member of the Indiana state legislature on the
Democratic ticket. From the Democratic party Debs moved into the
Populist party during the depression that began in 1893; by 1896, after
the Pullman strike, Debs was the choice of the radical wing of the
Populists for the presidential nomination. Thus Debs was well known
and respected by unionists throughout the country, as well as by hundreds of thousands of farmers, both northern and southern, who had
sympathized with Populism. In addition, although Debs was never a
deeply religious man, he was close to the Christian Socialists both in
style and in his personal morality. As a prolific editorialist, Debs remained known to a wide spectrum of reformers and radicals though
his writings in various socialist and labor periodicals in the years following the collapse of the ARU. And, of course, as an orator Debs was
unsurpassed in a period when public speaking was a high art and a
major form of public communication.

But although Debs could speak the mind of the party membership
more surely than any other single leader, with the possible exception
of Kate Richards O'Hare, he never guided the party or provided
day-to-day leadership in its organizational activities. Hero and symbol
of the movement, he preferred to remain above the organizational dis-
putes. Not until his release from prison in 1922—after serving three
years of a term for opposing the First World War—did Debs take a
seat on the National Executive Committee of the party; by then the
party was all but destroyed. At times in the prewar years this self-
abnegation created an unfortunate imbalance between the spirit (and
tactics) of the national leadership, from which Debs absented himself,

and the party membership. Control of the party organization fell into the hands of Berger, Hillquit, and their supporters for most of these years because of their strategic location and their organizational power. In addition, the better-known journalists and public figures, such as John Spargo, A. M. Simons, Robert Hunter, and J. Stitt Wilson, were often the "constructivist" candidates for the National Executive Committee and this helped consolidate control by the New York, Chicago, and Milwaukee leaders.

This is not to suggest that there were profound differences between Hillquit and Berger and Debs. Berger had converted Debs to Socialism while Debs was in jail as a result of his role in the Pullman strike, and the two remained friends for many years thereafter. In matters of principle Hillquit and Debs rarely differed. Both opposed dual unionism, sabotage, and the advocacy of violence; both actively opposed American participation in the First World War; both supported the Russian Revolution but opposed the policies of the Third International; both advocated industrial unionism. The principles that Debs and Hillquit held in common have led some historians to place them together as moderates, and in a broad sense this is correct. Yet, within the party, Debs is better understood as a left-winger, especially because of his rejection of Socialist participation in the AFL and because of his rapport with the Western radicals.

Thus while Hillquit, and even Berger, stood in principle for industrial unionism, Debs participated in the founding of the IWW and remained a member for the first few years. Largely because of his success in winning the labor movement in Milwaukee to Socialism, Berger believed strongly in working within the AFL and attempting to capture it for socialism. But throughout his Socialist days, Debs favored the formation of revolutionary industrial unions. He believed it useless to attempt to change the AFL, both because it was committed to interclass harmony and because it brought workers into conflict with one another through its craft organization. Any effort to influence the "rotten graft-infested" federation, Debs declared, would be "as useless as to spray a cesspool with attar of roses." Debs helped form the IWW in 1905 in the hope that it would organize the unorganized along industrial lines and become a socialist-oriented center for new and existing industrial unions. He dropped out of the IWW in 1908 after it split with Daniel De Leon (who set up his own IWW in Detroit) because it then began to repudiate socialist politics. By 1913 Debs was a bitter critic of the IWW's dual-union activities in the West Virginia coal fields, and of its opposition to socialist political action. Yet he still stood for a revolutionary industrial unionism. In 1914, during the Ludlow coal strike, Debs began a brief campaign for a new industrial federation, to be based on a merger of the Western Federation of Miners and the United Mine Workers Union. At the same time he praised the Detroit faction of the IWW and called for unification of the Socialist and Socialist Labor parties. But his calls elicited almost no interest, and Debs had nothing more to offer.

In principle, Debs's criticisms of the IWW were the same as Berger's, and conversely, Berger's abstract ideas about unions were the same as Debs's. But Berger had from the beginning been profoundly hostile to the IWW, and resentful of Debs's participation in it. Although always a forthright opponent of Gompers and the policies symbolized by Gompers' membership in the National Civic Federation, Berger argued strongly for working within the AFL. And, in fact, the major impact that the Socialists had on organized labor was within the ranks of various AFL unions. The party never did succeed in winning a majority of the AFL to Socialism, but at its high point in 1912 some one third of the delegates at the AFL convention voted for the Socialist opponent to Samuel Gompers; William H. Johnston was elected president of the International Association of Machinists, and the Socialists led several other internationals; Socialists were elected as presidents of State Federations of Labor in Pennsylvania, Illinois, and Wisconsin; and on Socialist initiative the United Mine Workers and the Carpenters both forced their leaders to withdraw from the National Civic Federation. Within the ranks of organized labor, and that meant the AFL and the Railroad Brotherhoods, the Socialist party had a strong following. At the same time, these unions had organized only a small percentage of the industrial working class, and except in coal mining and brewing, most of those organized were the skilled workers in their industries. Berger, Hillquit, and others stressed the need for close ties with the already organized workers; Debs was primarily concerned with organizing the unorganized.

Debs differed from his fellow socialists in his tactical approach to the labor movement, but agreed on the absolute necessity for revolutionaries to be active both in "politics" and in "economic" organizations. On this question he stood with the party against both Haywood, who remained the IWW's outstanding leader until he fled to Soviet Russia in 1921, and William Z. Foster, a syndicalist who quit the IWW to work within the AFL, and who led the packinghouse strike in Chicago in 1917 and the Great Steel Strike in 1919. Yet Debs also stood between these men and the party in the intensity of his belief that the desperate fight that the more militant unions were compelled to wage for their existence would drive them, willy-nilly, to become more and more revolutionary. In this respect Debs did not transcend the meaning of his own experience as a union man in the 1880s and 1890s and was unable fully to understand the significance of the National Civic Federation's efforts to convince the business

DEBS IN HISTORY / 171

community of the essentially conservative nature of trade unionism, whether along craft or industrial lines.*

Debs never fully understood the new liberalism of the Progressive Era or the changes that had occurred in the attitudes of the more sophisticated leaders of the large corporations between 1900 and 1918. His understanding of capitalist development followed from his own experience during the period of rapid industrialization in the last decades of the nineteenth century. In those years capital was scarce and the expansion of production capacity required the severest possible limitations on consumption. In that situation a fight for higher wages or shorter hours was much more directly a fight against the fundamental interests of the capitalist—and, therefore, the struggle for union recognition brought workers into direct opposition to the class interest of their employers. With the development of the large corporation and of the technology that made mass production possible, the contradiction between immediate consumption and the expansion of production capacity began to dissolve, particularly in the larger-scale and technologically more advanced industries. As this happened the threat posed by unionization became less fundamental, and in some cases the advantages it promised in the form of greater stability of the work force even outweighed the dangers of united action. In short, unionization, even on an industrial basis, began to lose whatever inherently revolutionary content it formerly had.

Neither Debs nor any other of the major leaders of the old Socialist party fully understood this process or its implications, and this lack of understanding was one of the things that prevented the continued growth and development of the party in the 1920s. In addition to that, the wartime experience itself had profoundly contradictory effects on the party and on Debs. The American Socialists, unlike almost all the other parties in the Second International, opposed the war even after their country entered the conflict directly. The party's militant opposition was highly popular among workers and farmers in most sections of the country, and in its popular appeal the party gained considerably, particularly in the elections of April and November 1917 (at which time, on the average, the party's vote increased about four times over the 1912–16 level). But along with its popular successes, indeed, in large part because of them, the party also suffered severe repression at the hands of the federal government, as well as state and local governments and many "private" (but governmentally encouraged) groups. Part of that experience included the removal from office of several elected officials—city councilmen in Cleveland,

* Leaders of the brewing industry, for example, were staunch supporters of the NCF even though the brewery workers were successfully organized along industrial lines.

state assemblymen in New York—for opposing the war and favoring the new Bolshevik regime in Russia.

These developments undermined many of the more optimistic ideas about the growth of Socialism into a majoritarian electoral movement that predominated in the party before the war. In addition, the policies of the Third (Moscow) International, formed early in 1919, further complicated the situation and divided the party. Like most of the other old-line party leaders, Debs strongly supported the Bolsheviks and opposed American intervention against the Revolution. In 1919 Debs declared that "from the crown of my head to the soles of my feet I am a Bolshevik and proud of it." Yet, like Hillquit, Berger, Kate Richards O'Hare, and others, Debs was opposed to the policies of the new International and particularly to the formation of the Communist parties in the United States. The issue was not support for the Bolsheviks, but the possibility of revolution in the United States in the immediate future. For the Bolsheviks this appeared as a matter of their own survival: socialist theory had always been that the revolution could occur only in the most advanced capitalist countries, since capitalist industrialization was understood to be a prerequisite to socialism. Lenin had believed this, too, until he saw the opportunity to take power in Russia as a result of the wartime crisis and the inability of all other groups, including the moderate socialists to govern. But Lenin believed that the revolution in Russia could survive only if it spread to the industrialized West. From 1917 to 1920 Bolshevik hopes for survival were in large part pinned on the anticipated spread of the Revolution, and the International was formed largely to speed that development. In the United States those who were to become Communists accepted the call of the International and stood for immediate insurrection. This policy was opposed by Debs, Hillquit, Berger, et al., as an impossibility.

Yet the split left the Socialists with its older leaders separated from the more militant and active youth, most of whom were swept up in the euphoria of the Bolshevik triumph. At the same time, Debs's voice and great moral influence were muffled because he was then in the Atlanta penitentiary, serving his term for opposing the war. By the time Debs was released from prison in December 1921, the split was two years in the past and antagonism between the Communists and Socialists was intense; the movement itself was in a shambles. From a membership of 109,000 before the split in 1919, the total membership of the Socialist and Communist parties in 1921 had fallen to some 30,000. The Socialist party itself was a shell: its state organizations and extensive press were all but destroyed; its enthusiasm and youth were gone; its comprehension of American society was less adequate than ever. The main asset it had left was the moral stature of Debs himself, and its legacy of having opposed the war.

But in the few years between his release from prison and his death, Debs was able to regain his old stature only fleetingly. After several months of rest and recuperation, Debs embarked on a speaking tour for the party. His initial meetings stirred excitement, drew overflow crowds almost everywhere, and led to spurts of renewed Socialist organization. In Minneapolis, for example, Debs spoke to an overflow crowd of five thousand and his appearance produced two new locals in the city. For a few months in the late winter and early spring of 1923, Debs's tour stimulated activity in the party. Many young people who had never heard him in the old days went to hear the aging leader, along with old-timers who wished to pay homage or recall the happier days of prewar radicalism. But the meetings did not inspire the younger members to renewed activity. In 1924, Bertha Hale White, the party's National Secretary, admitted that since his release from prison, she had not been able to arrange a second meeting for Debs "that was not a bitter disappointment to him." He did not seem to realize, she wrote, that his imprisonment was "an old story," and that changes in his text were necessary. "The war is over long since, the old speeches will not do," she told Debs. But although the audiences expected "a new theme" and the party's own members were becoming dissatisfied, Debs had nothing new to say. He never drew a large second crowd in any city, and soon after his tour ended the party settled back into its previous condition. For the next three years Debs actively worked for the party when he was not too ill to do so, but there was to be no revival for either. In October of 1926 Debs died. His death symbolized the fate of the party.

Afterword

The historian's treatment of Debs varies with his own philosophy of history. Arthur M. Schlesinger, Jr., has for many years been the nation's major Vital Center historian. Historian, presidential advisor, and Democratic political figure, Schlesinger, as one author once put it, writes as he votes. In his classic *The Age of Jackson*, Schlesinger wrote that "liberalism in America has been ordinarily the movement on the part of the other sections of society to restrain the power of the business community."

The statement assumes that a popular movement, opposed by business, continually arises in America to challenge the one-sided power of large corporate business. But new historical research by a generation of revisionists has all but wiped out this assumption. William Appleman Williams, Gabriel Kolko, James Weinstein, Murray N. Rothbard, and others have argued that liberalism has actually been the ideology of dominant business groups, and that they have in reality favored state intervention to supervise corporate activity.

Schlesinger, because of the definition he offers, is able to treat Eugene V. Debs as another "liberal," or as a self-proclaimed socialist who was great only because he was really part of the current of liberalism. Debs, however, did not favor any form of regulatory activity, especially those proposals introduced by corporate bodies like the National Civic Federation. He favored expropriation of private property, and yet he is transformed in Schlesinger's essay into a harmless liberal. Schlesinger, moreover, writes that the Socialists found themselves isolated when they developed their antiwar position. Actually, their popularity increased throughout the nation, and this was accurately reflected by the increase in Socialist votes at the polls.

Schlesinger ends by honoring Debs as a democrat "who held firmly to democratic traditions of change through debate and consent." Debs is thus put into the conventional parliamentarian framework: another politician who happened to be a socialist. Nowhere does one find an indication that Debs worried about his party becoming a force for "bourgeois reform," or that Debs advocated the right of armed self-defense by workers, a concept followed in today's world by those black militants gathered in the Black Panther party.

Writing in the same manner, H. Wayne Morgan has Debs disavowing "the more extreme socialist tendencies," neglecting the context of Debs's total commitment to revolution and his opposition to the bourgeois order. Morgan also depicts Debs as a man within the tradition of "liberal politics." Thus Debs is sadly remembered by conservative historians for all that he disavowed during his lifetime. Morgan confuses Debs's tactical opposition to the program of "anarchistic individualists" with a supposed hope that the new order could be attained "by working within the existing system." Debs becomes an American variation of Eduard Bernstein's Marxian Revisionist, rather than an independent class-conscious revolutionary. Finally, Morgan reveals his own bias when he attributes Debs's failure to the essential vitality of American capitalism, confusing the ability of capitalism to continue with its being a sufficient explanation for the failure of American radicalism. It is true that the Socialist party entered a period of decline, but as James Weinstein convincingly argues, this had as much to do with its own understanding of America and with the response to the Bolshevik Revolution as with the supposed viability of corporation capitalism.

Understandably, the Socialist and radical historians treat Debs in a more sympathetic and comprehensive manner. One does not find in their writings about Debs the simplistic liberal distortions that appear in Schlesinger and Morgan, but they differ in other respects. Ray Ginger has written what will remain the classic biography of Debs. Ginger argues that Debs hurt his own goals by favoring revolutionary industrial unionism, since that decision isolated him from organized labor. Similarly, he sees Debs's refusal to cooperate with reform parties and his treatment of racial prejudice as a purely class issue as harmful.

Socialist author Bert Cochran agrees only on the last point. He argues that Debs missed his chance to support revolutionary socialists and to straighten them out on the issue of direct action and syndicalism. But Cochran does not view Debs's decision to support the IWW in 1905 as an error, since he does not believe it was predetermined that industrial union organization had to fail. His criticism is that the IWW was doomed, because it was "decidedly limited" as a cross between a union and a revolutionary party.

On this question of trade unionism, David Herreshoff puts forth a highly unorthodox theory. Concentrating on Debs's fight for industrial unionism, Herreshoff claims that Debs was an ally of Daniel De Leon, the noted American Marxist who led the Socialist Labor party. He cites Debs's emphasis on class consciousness and his opposition to any socialist alliances with reactionary trade unions. Hence Herreshoff treats Debs as a De Leonite, a Socialist who opposed reform fights and who stood in unity with the much despised De Leon. Herreshoff stands alone as the only socialist historian to discuss Debs in this manner.

In the final essay in this collection, James Weinstein offers the most fruitful considerations for an understanding and comprehension of the eventual failure of Debsian socialism. Socialism failed not because of a supposed middle-class psychology held by workers or because the capitalist system was stable and had no basic inherent conflicts. Rather, even Socialists as astute as Debs were unable to comprehend the way in which corporate capitalism had changed the system.

Corporate capitalism had put power in the hands of a new so-phisticated group of leaders, a national class that instituted a new political system, corporate liberalism. This system changed the nature of industrial reality. With the maturity of industrial machine pro-duction, corporations could afford to give workers a higher return for their labor power. The worker no longer resembled the economically deprived proletarian of the nineteenth century. As Marx had argued, more and more would be produced by fewer and fewer people, and the system would be able to give adequate material compensation to those who ran the machinery. In such circumstances, unionism was no longer a fundamental threat to the system. Hence socialists who believed in the possibility of workers becoming radicalized through union struggles would soon find that they had failed. Some employers, like the sophisticated Gerard Swope of General Electric, even favored the creation of industrial unions in industry to achieve stabilization and efficiency. This was a possibility never envisioned in the compre-hension of Marxism held by Debs and the early Socialists.

Debs, despite his greatness, attempted to build a Socialist movement on a poor theoretical foundation. All that was left was his shining personal commitment, along with a thoroughly inadequate understand-ing of how corporate capitalism had transformed the system of ex-ploitation. It is no accident that historians are prone to remember Debs for his humanity and his dedication to deeply held principles, when it is so obvious that his most cherished dream did not come to pass. Historical perspective allows us to see that Debs could not have had the understanding needed to make complete sense out of capital-ism during the period of transition to the new corporate era. It re-mains for those of us living in the age of corporate capitalism's maturity to apply ourselves rigorously to this task.

Bibliographical Note

Readers seeking to learn more about Eugene V. Debs would do best to begin with some of the now standard accounts of the development of American Socialism. These include Daniel Bell, "The Background and Development of Marxian Socialism in the United States," in Donald D. Egbert and Stow Persons, eds., *Socialism and American Life* (Princeton, 1952); Ira Kipnis, *The American Socialist Movement: 1897–1912* (New York, 1952); Howard H. Quint, *The Forging of American Socialism: Origins of the Modern Movement* (Columbia, South Carolina, 1953); Theodore Draper, *The Roots of American Communism,* (New York, 1957); and David A. Shannon, *The Socialist Party of America* (New York, 1955).

A forceful challenge to the concept that American Socialism had no roots in American life, and that it declined after 1912 because of the Socialist party's opposition to World War I and its irrelevance in the face of Wilsonian liberal reform, is to be found in two works that substantially alter the traditional analysis of American socialism: James Weinstein, *The Decline of Socialism in America, 1912–1925* (New York, 1967); and James Weinstein, "Socialism's Hidden Heritage: Scholarship Reinforces Political Mythology," in James Weinstein and David W. Eakins, eds., *For A New America: Essays in History and Politics from 'Studies on the Left' 1959–1967* (New York, 1970), pp. 221–52.

The literature on Debs and Debsian socialism is understandably large. The best account of Debs's entire life is to be found in the now classic biography: Ray Ginger, *The Bending Cross, A Biography of Eugene Victor Debs* (New Brunswick, New Jersey, 1949). Far less satisfactory is the essentially derivative account contained in H. Wayne Morgan, *Eugene V. Debs: Socialist for President* (Syracuse, N.Y., 1962). Grouped around Debs's five presidential campaigns between 1900 and 1920, Morgan's book suffers from an uncritical acceptance of the traditional thesis advanced by Kipnis and Bell regarding the decline of American socialism. A more provocative yet scholarly analysis is offered by David Herreshoff, *American Disciples of Marx: from the Age of Jackson to the Progressive Era* (Detroit, 1967). Two sympathetic and critical accounts of Debs are: Bert Cochran, "The Achievement of Debs," in Harvey Goldberg, ed., *American Radicals, Some Problems and Personalities* (New York, 1957); and a chapter in Charles A. Madison, *Critics and Crusaders* (New York, 1947).

Readers wishing to turn directly to Debs's own writings and speeches may consult: Bruce Rogers, ed., *Debs: His Life, Writings and Speeches* (Girard, Kansas, 1908); and Joseph M. Bernstein, ed., *Writings and Speeches of Eugene V. Debs* (New York, 1948). The latter volume covers Debs's entire life and prints almost all of his most important statements. Both books, unfortunately, are out of print and difficult to obtain. A new volume of Debs's speeches and writings, with an introduction by the American Trotskyist leader, James

A. Cannon has just been published: Gene Tussey, ed., *Eugene V. Debs Speaks* (New York, 1970). Debs himself published one book, an account of his impressions of prison life, *Walls and Bars* (Chicago, 1927). His writings are also to be found in David Karsner, *Debs, His Authorized Life and Letters* (New York, 1919); and David Karsner, *Talks with Debs in Terre Haute* (New York, 1922).

Debs's manuscript material, unfortunately, is scattered in many different libraries throughout the country. The most important collections are the Debs manuscripts in the Indiana State Library, Indianapolis; the Debs collection in the Joseph A. Labadie Archives at the University of Michigan; the Debs Foundation in Terre Haute; and the immense Debs collection at the Tamiment Institute Library of New York University. This collection contains all the personal material that Debs handed to the Rand School of Social Science before his death. Other peripheral collections that contain both references to Debs and information on Socialist party politics include the Morris Hillquit manuscripts and the Daniel De Leon manuscripts at the State Historical Society of Wisconsin in Madison; the Socialist party manuscripts at Duke University; and the Samuel Gompers Letter-Books at the Library of Congress, Washington, D.C.

An extensive Debs bibliography, including a list of significant Debs articles which appeared in different newspapers and magazines, as well as a listing of articles about Debs and American socialism, is to be found in Ray Ginger's *The Bending Cross*. A new edition of this book, which reproduces the original footnotes and bibliography, has been issued in paperback under the title *Eugene V. Debs, The Making of an American Radical* (New York, 1962).

Index

A

American Federation of Labor (AFL), 4, 29, 52, 101, 109, 146, 161, 167, 169, 170
American Labor Union, 108, 109
American Railway Union, 1, 11–14, 17, 18, 19, 99, 107, 108, 133, 144, 155, 160, 163, 168
Agents provocateurs, 40
Anarchism, 105
Anthony, Susan B., 80
Appeal to Reason, 101, 159

B

Baker, Charles, 102
Bellamy, Edward, 2, 19
Benson, Allen L., 4
Berger, Victor, 2, 5, 19, 116, 117, 120, 122, 144, 157, 160, 170, 172
Billings, Warren K., 101
Blatchford, Robert, 19, 144
Bohn, Frank, 38, 41
Bolshevism, 85–88
Brotherhood of Locomotive Firemen, 1, 15–16, 99, 107–8
Broun, Heywood, on Debs, 40–42
Brown, John, 39, 115, 116
Bryan, William Jennings, 21, 109

C

Campbell–Bannerman, Henry, 113
Capitalism, 21, 22, 59, 78, 87, 118, 124–125, 128, 130
Christian Socialists, 167, 168
Civic Federation (see National Civic Federation)
Class struggle, Negro, 60–63
Cochran, Bert, on Debs, 159–62
Comintern, 6, 148, 172
Communist Manifesto (Marx), 38
Comrade, The, 15
Cook County Jail, Chicago, Ill., 18

Co-Operative Commonwealth, The (Gronlund), 2
Cox, James M., 147
Craft unionism, 4

D

Daily Worker, 148
Darrow, Clarence, 18
Das Kapital (Marx), 100, 144
De Leon, Daniel, 145, 163–66, 169
Declaration of Independence, 47

E

Eastman, Max, on Debs, 133–38
Economic unionism, 43
Ekrich, Arthur A., Jr., 6
Espionage Act (1917), 5, 66, 82, 102, 133, 147
Executive Miner's Union, 22n.

F

Field, Eugene, 145
Flynn, Helen Gurley, on Debs, 98–103
Foster, William Z., 160, 170
Franklin, Benjamin, 80
Friends of the Soviet Union, 102

G

Garrison, William Lloyd, 80
General Managers' Association, 13
Ginger, Ray, on Debs, 155–58
Goebel, George H., 149
Goldman, Emma, on Debs, 104–5
Gompers, Samuel, 4, 26, 29, 49, 106, 146, 155, 170
Great Northern Railroad, 1, 12, 99
Gronlund, Lawrence, 2, 19
Guards, mine, 46